BOOKKEEPING

A Beginner's Guide to Accounting
and Bookkeeping For Small
Businesses

BY MICHAEL KANE

consult a licensed professional before attempting any techniques outlined in this book.

By reading this document, the reader agrees that under no circumstances are the author responsible for any losses, direct or indirect, which are incurred as a result of the use of the information contained within this document, including, but not limited to, —errors, omissions, or inaccuracies.

Table of Contents

INTRODUCTION

The word bookkeeping and accounting are accounting terminologies. If you are an accountant, business owner, business administrator, etc. you should understand what these terms mean. Bookkeeping and accounting are very important aspects of business activities. Although some people use these two terms, interchangeably, accounting, and bookkeeping have different meanings.

If you want to run a small business, you need to have an understanding of bookkeeping and accounting. Bookkeeping and accounting have a lot of benefits for small business owners. A successful small business is the result of accurate bookkeeping and accounting, and understanding the practices of bookkeeping is very important for the smooth operation of your business.

The practices of accounting and bookkeeping are not difficult to understand. This is the ultimate guide to bookkeeping and accounting for beginners. It explains everything you need to understand these subjects.

Several small businesses do well in sales, advertising, building good teams, and customer services. However, these businesses have issues when it comes to the aspect of bookkeeping and accounting. A business will run well if transactions are recorded, and different types of accounts are kept properly.

You can only evaluate the performance of your businesses if you practice the art of bookkeeping and accounting. Bookkeeping and accounting help organize your finances and evaluate your business's performance. As a business owner, you must have a financial understanding of how your business operates.

A good bookkeeping and accounting system helps you to plan for the future. As a small business owner, you can decide to do your bookkeeping yourself or hire someone to help you do it. The primary aspect of the accounting system in an organization is bookkeeping.

Some people underrate the importance of bookkeeping in businesses. The art of bookkeeping keeps your business on the right track. If you do not understand the bookkeeping and accounting system, your business might fail. With an effective bookkeeping and accounting system, you will understand and plan your business.

If you are willing to learn the art of bookkeeping, this book will help you achieve your goal. Bookkeeping and accounting will help you to keep a good track of your sales, purchases, expenses, profits, bad debts, etc. One of the keys to operating a successful business is effective bookkeeping and accounting.

Regardless of the type of business you are operating, the accounting and bookkeeping requirements are the same. When it comes to accounting and bookkeeping, you need to decide the accounting software you'd like to use, the accounting method suitable for you, understand how transactions are recorded, and establish different types of accounts.

You need to ask yourself some questions before you start managing your business. Questions like: "How will I record my transactions?" "What type of accounting software should I opt for?" "Can I manage my business myself or hire someone to do it for me?" "What kind of accounting method should I use?"

Bookkeeping and accounting system can be very engaging and stressful if you do not understand the basics of bookkeeping and accounting. Knowing the right thing to do is one of those things that will help you run a successful business. There are different aspects of bookkeeping you need to learn for the smooth running of your business.

Keeping up-to-date financial records of your small business makes you know how your business is fairing and what steps need to be taken for improvement.

Effective bookkeeping shows how you can manage your business. The financial performance of your business helps to evaluate the success of your business.

Bookkeeping and accounting systems can be seen as a report card. A student's report card at the end of the term reveals the overall performance of that student; this is the same function of bookkeeping and accounting in small businesses. You can only perform better when you are aware of previous performance.

Why Businesses are Successful

There is no doubt that an effective bookkeeping and accounting system is the key to running a successful business. The art of bookkeeping and accounting systems is to understand the financial aspects of your business. A business will fail if it doesn't maintain good records of its transactions. A business can do well in all other aspects, but if it fails in its financial aspects, such a business will crumble.

The success of a business is determined by several factors, of which bookkeeping and accounting is a very important one. Success in business is not determined by how many sales you made or the profit you generated but by how you kept track of your transactions. The question is, how will you realize the profits generated and the sales you made if you do not keep records of your transactions?

It is only when you keep up-to-date financial records of your transactions that you can determine the performance of your business. A business is operated to generate profit, but this goal can be hindered if one fails to maintain an effective bookkeeping and accounting system.

The art of bookkeeping is an essential aspect of a business. Some small businesses failed - not because they did not make sales, or they failed to produce good products - but they failed to maintain an effective bookkeeping and accounting system.

We do not just emphasize the importance of bookkeeping and accounting because we want to force business owners to do it. The importance of bookkeeping and accounting is explained because it is vital for becoming a successful business owner and is important for both small and large businesses.

No matter how small your business is, you need to keep good track of all transactions. When you operate a business, you will certainly carry out some transactions, and these transactions should not be left unrecorded. This book was written to explain how to appropriately track those transactions.

Businesses operate well when effective bookkeeping and accounting systems are managed. To understand the art of bookkeeping, one needs to understand some basic concepts. A business should be operated to achieve success, not only to make a profit.

The Difference Between Accounting and Bookkeeping

Although the two concepts have been explained above, one needs to explain these two concepts broadly. When we talk about bookkeeping, we mean the day-to-day records of financial transactions carried out in a business or organization. Bookkeeping is an aspect of financial accounting. Most financial statements or reports are derived from bookkeeping.

Accounting involves summarizing financial transactions that have already been recorded. The primary goal of accounting is the preparation of financial reports or statements. There are different branches of accounting; these include management accounting, cost accounting, auditing, etc.

Accounting deals with summarizing bookkeeping results in annual financial reports. Bookkeeping is the fundamentals of accounting. This simply means that without bookkeeping, there will be nothing accounted for. Bookkeeping keeps track of financial transactions that all financial statements and reports are derived from.

Bookkeeping involves determining and recording financial transactions, preparing ledger accounts, and making trial balances. Accounting involves identifying, recording, and summarizing financial transactions, preparing financial reports, and analyzing financial statements. Financial accounting helps business owners, stakeholders, and investors to determine the financial position of an organization.

Bookkeeping is carried out according to the accounting conventions and concepts. Financial statements are not part of the bookkeeping process; they are derived from bookkeeping by accountants. Bookkeeping is performed by a bookkeeper, while a well-skilled accountant performs accounting. Bookkeeping and accounting are two different concepts, although they are related.

The Role of a Bookkeeper

A bookkeeper performs the following roles:

- Makes journal entries for all business transactions carried out.

- Prepares a trial balance.

- Records the inflow and outflow of cash in a business.

- Maintains and balances general ledgers, subsidiaries, and historical accounts.

- Responsible for preparing bank reconciliations.

- Issues invoices to debtors.

- Files tax returns.

- Ensures compliance with accounting principles.

- Serves as the middleman between a business and its customers.

- Pay accounts on the business's behalf.

Bookkeepers work in various organizations. Bookkeepers do not necessarily need to acquire formal education. To be a successful bookkeeper, you need to be knowledgeable about bookkeeping skills and major financial topics.

How to Run a Successful Small Business

Running a successful business is the topmost priority of small business owners. A business becomes successful not only because of the capital used for starting the business but the strategies and critical decisions made in the business. Below are tips on how you can run a successful business.

- Set up a trading strategy

A trading strategy is like an outline that shows the criteria for money management in a business. Technological advancement has made this easier for businesses today. You can evaluate a business idea before taking the risk with your capital. This is also referred to as back-testing. This method helps business owners to decide if a business plan will work for a business.

Once you have a business plan and you have tested its feasibility, and it reveals positive results, then you can use the plan in your business. Ensure that you stick to the business plan you have designed for your business.

- Utilize the Internet to your advantage

There are so many businesses in the world. Your business is not the only one that exists as there are several businesses similar to yours. You can make use of technology like the Internet to get more business strategies and understand what will work for your type of business. By getting the necessary information from the Internet and using it to your advantage, this is a way of promoting your business.

Information is key. Business owners should learn more every day. It is very important that you understand what the markets need and then deliver exactly what they want. Good research enables small business owners to know facts about businesses.

- Establish a trading strategy based on facts

As a business owner, you can take your time to set up a business strategy that is based on known facts. Nobody wants to build his or her business based on myths. Do not be in a hurry to achieve your plans, but take it slowly.

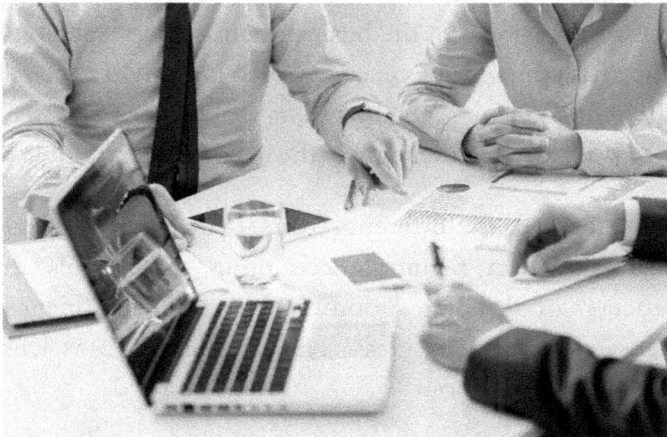

CHAPTER 1

BASICS OF BOOKKEEPING

You must have heard of the word bookkeeping on one or two occasions. In the business world, bookkeeping is not a new thing. It has existed for so long. When we talk about bookkeeping, the first thing that comes to people's minds is that bookkeeping is the art of keeping books.

Bookkeeping is different from that; it is a broad terminology in financial accounting that entails the process of keeping good records of all financial transactions in a business. This chapter explains what bookkeeping is about.

What is Bookkeeping?

Bookkeeping is an accounting concept that refers to the act of recording, verifying, retrieving, storing, and organizing the financial transactions carried out in a business or organization. Bookkeeping is sometimes called record keeping. Bookkeeping is an aspect of financial accounting that deals with recording financial transactions and events in a business or organization.

Bookkeeping can be carried out manually or with the use of bookkeeping software. The principles of financial accounting lie in keeping accurate and up-to-date records. Therefore, bookkeeping is the basis of financial accounting. It is the source of information for most of the accounting systems.

Bookkeepers are trained to use their analytical skills in recording financial transactions because most accounting information is sourced from these financial records. There are different aspects of financial accounting; these include bookkeeping, auditing, share valuation, financial forecasting, etc. Without bookkeeping, none of these aspects can function; bookkeeping is the backbone of financial accounting.

Bookkeeping provides well-detailed and accurate information from which other accounts like balance sheets, trading, profit and loss accounts, ledgers, and depreciation, among others, are prepared. Without bookkeeping, none of these accounts can be prepared. Bookkeeping is a vital aspect of financial accounting.

Each financial transaction in a business must be recorded. There are ways in which these transactions are recorded. Bookkeeping does not only involve the recording of figures, but it also records financial transactions and events. Bookkeeping is essential for a business to thrive.

The concepts of bookkeeping and accounting are often used interchangeably, although they are separate. Bookkeeping is a vital aspect of accounting, while accounting is the general way of managing a business's finances. A person who studies bookkeeping is referred to as a bookkeeper.

A bookkeeper must understand some accounting principles and how transactions should be recorded. The process of recording and organizing transactions is called bookkeeping. Accounting is a broader concept and should not be mistaken for bookkeeping. Bookkeeping is simply an aspect of financial accounting.

Gone are the days when bookkeeping was done manually, the process of recording and organizing financial transactions has been made easier in today's world. Bookkeeping can be carried out via computer software. There are several programs used for recording and organizing transactions.

Keeping accurate and up-to-date records of all transactions is vital in bookkeeping. Bookkeeping is useless if the transactions recorded are not accurate. The most important factor in bookkeeping is accuracy. Bookkeeping is done to offer well-detailed and accurate information required to create accounting statements.

The Importance of Bookkeeping

Bookkeeping is very important in small businesses. Bookkeeping is a core aspect of accounting. It is important in all businesses and organizations regardless of the type or size of businesses operated. Businesses can fail because of poor bookkeeping. Below are the reasons why bookkeeping is important.

Organization

When bookkeeping is defined, the word organization is used. Bookkeeping deals with the recording and the organizing of transactions. The organization is very important when running a business. A successful business owner is one that is very organized in all activities carried out.

Bookkeeping helps you gain access to the necessary details regarding your business. For instance, if you need some details about sales, an effective bookkeeping system will help you get the necessary information you need. Some parties, like employees, Internal Revenue Service, customers, lenders, researchers, auditors, and investors, are interested in your financial records. Providing these parties with accurate and well-detailed information can help your business.

The Internal Revenue Service can penalize you, as a business owner, if you refuse to provide the required, necessary records. Investors may stop investing in your business if they lack access to your records. Staying organized and up to date with your bookkeeping will help maintain a good working relationship between you and your investors.

An effective bookkeeping system will help you have access to the necessary information required from your business. If you are disorganized with your records, this can cause a big problem for you. Book organization is very important if you want a smooth running business.

Decision Making

If you want to make wise decisions in your business, then you need to practice effective bookkeeping. Bookkeeping helps you to make better decisions in your business. As a business owner, you need to make good decisions that will have a positive effect on your business. A bad decision can ruin your business and leave you with no choice than to shut down your business.

Decision making is a vital aspect of a business. You cannot make good decisions if you don't know anything about bookkeeping. Bookkeeping reveals areas where a business is lagging. With this information, you can set new goals to fix the problems in these areas.

To make a good decision, you need to know the necessary details that will help your business. Some businesses crumble because of bad decisions. If you keep good track of records in your business, you can make decisions based on these accurate and up to date records.

Budget Creation

A budget is necessary for all businesses and organizations. Even a country creates financial budgets yearly. A budget is a financial statement that shows the estimated income and expenditure. It is a way of creating a financial plan on how you will spend money. A budget helps you to plan for the future.

Creating a budget is very important for your business. When you have a correct estimate of expenses and income, it will help your business perform well. Creating a budget helps you make good plans. Carrying out efficient bookkeeping will help you create feasible budgets.

Good Planning

Good planning is an important practice in bookkeeping. Bookkeeping reveals the past performance of a business or organization, and by evaluating this, proper planning can be made for the future.

Bookkeeping helps you create strategic plans that will help your business. Bookkeeping helps you to plan for taxation. It also provides the necessary details to categorize expenses and revenues to help estimate future costs and profit.

Bookkeeping helps your certified public accountant determine which expenses are more favorable. For instance, providing lunch during conferences in your organization can be favorable to your business in terms of taxation.

Taxation

Every year, your business will most likely have to pay tax. Most businesses do not have accurate records, so the tax filing process is inefficient. With an efficient bookkeeping system, your financial details can be ready for tax filing.

During tax filing, bookkeeping provides your accountant with what is required for filing taxes. Accountants prepare tax reports to determine the tax payable to local and federal authorities. Accountants can only prepare tax reports with the help of an efficient bookkeeping system.

Profit Realization

Bookkeeping helps you to realize the profits you make in your business. For instance, bookkeeping records the income you generate in your business, and the income statement is derived from your bookkeeping. Calculating the profits made from your business helps you know the performance of your business.

Bookkeeping helps you to track the growth of your business. The amount of profit you realize from your business shows how your business is fairing. The trading, profit and loss account is derived from income and expenditure accounts in bookkeeping.

Good Reporting to Investors

Investors need accurate details of your business' financial transactions because they have a stake in the business. Investors have rights in your business and can make certain decisions. They need to know how their money is utilized, if the business is realizing profits or not, and what is needed to be done to improve the business.

Bookkeeping reveals all these things. With a good bookkeeping system in practice, your investors will have a clear picture of your business. The profit and loss account, which is obtained through bookkeeping, reveals the income generated and the loss incurred in the business. Bookkeeping helps you to give accurate reports to your investors.

Good Financial Management

The importance of bookkeeping can never be underestimated. It helps business owners maintain good cash flow. As a business owner, bookkeeping helps you take charge of the finances in your business. Bookkeeping analyzes your business' finances to ensure they are being managed properly. The only way to determine the overall performance of your business is by keeping good records of all financial transactions.

With bookkeeping, you can make balance sheets, trial balance, trading, ledger, profit, and loss accounts. The performance of a business can only be evaluated by making a comparison between these accounts.

Peace of Mind

One problem faced by business owners is how to practice effective and accurate bookkeeping. With an effective bookkeeping system in place, you'll have nothing to worry about if your records are requested by the IRS. You will not be scared when your investors, clients, the IRS, or banks ask for your financial statement. With a sound bookkeeping system, you do not need to have sleepless nights again.

Easy Auditing

If you maintain an effective bookkeeping system, your auditors will be grateful to you. Keeping good records of your transactions makes auditing as simple as ABC. If your books are well organized, auditing will be made easier and faster.

Auditors require certain documents from you, and if you cannot figure out where these documents are, your auditors can become frustrated. For instance, if your business is being audited by the Internal Revenue Service and your books are disorganized, you can be penalized.

Types of Bookkeeping

There are two major types of bookkeeping: single entry and double entry.

Single-Entry Bookkeeping

Small businesses mostly utilize the single-entry system of bookkeeping. It is easy and simple to carry out. Due to its simple nature, it is typically used for uncomplicated and small transactions. This system of bookkeeping keeps records of business expenses, cash sales, and profits.

Businesses having many capital transactions accounts receivable, and accounts payable do not utilize this system of bookkeeping. The single-entry system allows you to view all the expenses incurred and the income generated for a period. This system of bookkeeping is suitable for sole proprietors.

In the single-entry system of bookkeeping, there is only one entry for every transaction carried out. You record all entries in a column. In this system, you can prepare a two-column ledger, in which one is for expenses, and the other is for revenue. This system of bookkeeping does not record accounts such as accounts receivable, inventory, and the likes.

The single-entry can be used to calculate the profits realized in a business. Transactions in the single-entry system do not have a debit and credit side. This system of bookkeeping can make it difficult to trace revenue and expenses since they are all recorded in just one entry.

Double-Entry System

Both small and big businesses use the double-entry system of bookkeeping. The double entry system is sometimes call a "T-account" because the entries take on the shape of the letter "T" on the page. In the double-entry system, there are two columns for every account. There are two separate entries for every transaction carried out. There is a column for the debit account and another column for the credit account.

This system of bookkeeping is utilized by businesses that have complex transactions, organizations, or businesses that have accounts receivable, accounts payable, and inventory. Any income received is recorded on the debit side of the account, while expenses are recorded on the credit side of the account.

For example, if a customer pays you, it is recorded as income and also recorded in the account of the customer. If a transaction is carried out, you need to know which transaction is an income and which is an expense.

If an organization needs to pay a creditor, two accounts will be opened, the cash account and the customer's account. If you want to keep a check of your liability accounts, you need to utilize the double-entry system. In this system, a business owner can easily calculate the loss and profit of the organization. It also makes it easy to make financial statements directly from the books.

CHAPTER 2

TIPS ON BOOKKEEPING FOR SMALL BUSINESS

Small businesses need bookkeeping and accounting for their smooth running. No matter how small your business is, you need bookkeeping and accounting. Most small business owners manage their accounting systems themselves.

Small business accounting is easy and simple to do. There are small businesses that practice efficient bookkeeping and accounting systems. This chapter discusses the basics of small business accounting and what you need to do if you are a small business owner.

Steps on Small Business Bookkeeping

There are certain things you need to know and certain steps that need to be followed when operating small business accounting.

Understand Business Accounts

In small business accounting, all transactions carried out are recorded in different accounts. As a business owner, you need to know that there are five types of accounts. These accounts are equity, liabilities, expenses, assets, and revenues.

- Equity: This refers to the amount remaining after your liabilities have been subtracted from your assets.

- Liabilities: Liabilities are debts or financial obligations owed by an organization or business. Examples of liabilities are loans, accounts payable, customer deposits, etc.

- Expenses: Expenses are also called expenditures. They refer to the outflow of cash from businesses to acquire items or pay for services. Examples are the payment of utilities, salaries, etc.

- Assets: These are known to be resources and cash a business owns. These resources have economic value that later on provides financial benefit for a business. Examples are real estate, supplies, inventory, etc.

- Revenue: Revenue is also known as income. This refers to the in-flow of cash in a business; it is usually obtained through sales.

Accounting and bookkeeping start by creating the necessary accounts to record each transaction. You need to understand the accounts explained above very well before you start recording transactions in your business.

Open a Business Account

You need to open a bank account. This is very important since you now understand the various types of accounts in financial accounting. In the old days, a book known as a general ledger was used to record charts of accounts. These days, most organizations utilize different computer software to keep track of accounts. It can be a hard copy or virtual record; it is still regarded as the general ledger.

The cheapest software to use is spreadsheet software. A general ledger can be created using three methods: desktop accounting bookkeeping software, spreadsheet software, and cloud-based bookkeeping software. Desktop bookkeeping is good bookkeeping software that requires an up-front fee.

If you are utilizing cloud-based bookkeeping software like Wave, QuickBooks Online, you need to subscribe monthly, but the subscription is not as expensive as desktop software. You should open your business accounts to keep good records of all of your financial transactions.

Choose your Preferred Bookkeeping Method

There are different methods of bookkeeping. You can decide to use software for your bookkeeping or do it manually. You can use the single-entry or double-entry bookkeeping system. You can hire a professional to record your transactions, or you can do it yourself.

Before you start bookkeeping, you need to decide the best bookkeeping system you would like to practice. If you are operating a small business, the single-entry bookkeeping is ideal for you. However, the most common bookkeeping system used is double-entry bookkeeping. In the double-entry bookkeeping system, any transaction recorded in an account needs to be recorded in another account as an opposite entry.

In this system of bookkeeping, for every transaction, you are required to record two entries. There is always a debit (Dr) and a credit (Cr) column for all entries. The debit is always on the left side while the credit occupies the right side.

A double-entry bookkeeping system requires more tasks than single-entry bookkeeping. With this system, your books will be balanced, provided that you keep accurate and up-to-date records. It easier for you to know how much profit you realize if you use the double-entry bookkeeping system.

Record all Financial Transactions

The business accounts you created are not for fun; they are used for recording every financial transaction you carry out. After creating your business accounts and you have chosen the system of bookkeeping you want, the next step is to ensure you record all financial transactions properly.

An efficient bookkeeping system is one that contains well-detailed and up-to-date transactions. If you fail to record every financial transaction, then your bookkeeping is not efficient. Make sure you record each credit and debit transaction in the right column. If you fail to do this, your balances will not tally, and you cannot close your books.

If you are recording a transaction, the first thing you do is determine which account should be recorded on the debit side and the credit side. For instance, you purchased a new vehicle for your business for $20,000 and paid for it in cash. Two accounts will be opened: a cash account and equipment account. Since your cash is decreasing and your equipment is increasing, you will debit your equipment account and credit the cash account.

Close your Books

You must close your book at the end of the month or year. Balancing your books will help you determine your profits and where you need to make certain adjustments.

Your errors will be revealed if you are the type that keeps inaccurate information. The total of debits and credit accounts must tally when you are balancing your books.

If your books are well balanced, it shows that you have recorded all financial transactions properly. If the debit and credit side have different values, you'll have to go through your journal entries to locate the errors.

Make Financial Reports

If your books are well balanced, then you can make financial statements or reports from your books. Most financial statements like balance sheet, cash flow statement, profit, and loss statement are all derived from bookkeeping.

Making financial reports enables you to evaluate the financial performance of your business. The profit and loss statement, which is also known as an income statement, helps you to know how much profit realized or loss incurred in your business. It reveals the in-flow and out-flow of cash to and from your business.

The cash flow statement is just like the Profit and Loss account; it excludes non-cash items like depreciation. Cash flow statements reveal the aspect your business is spending on and where it is earning income. Bookkeeping helps you to make financial statements, and these statements can help you make financial decisions.

Store your Records Securely

Recording all financial transactions properly helps small businesses and makes it much easier to create financial records and reports. Keep your records in a secure place. You do not want a situation where you have to start looking for your records.

If you do not know about the principles of financial accounting, you can hire a professional to help you keep good records of your transactions. Ensure all your books are kept safely to prevent future problems and make sure you have backups.

The Fundamentals of Small Business Accounting

Every business needs to keep good records of its financial transactions to evaluate its overall performance on a yearly or monthly basis. There are certain principles you need to understand about small business accounting.

Accounting is a much broader concept that entails recording financial transactions and creating financial statements. Below are certain things you need to understand when operating small business accounting.

Open a Bank Account

As a business owner, you need to open a bank account where you will keep your business income. You cannot hold all your income as cash; you need to put some in your bank account. If you create a separate bank account for your records, it will make your work easier for you during tax filing.

Businesses like partnerships, corporations, and LLCs are required to hold a separate bank account. Sole proprietors do not need to operate a separate account.

Open bank accounts that will make it easy for you to plan for taxes and organize funds.

For example, you can create a savings account and spend a proportion of each payment as your tax. Limited liability companies and corporations are legally required to operate a separate account and utilize a separate credit card to prevent mixing up personal and business assets.

Ensure you use your business name to open your business account. Ensure you open a bank account for your business, and your business should be registered with your province or state.

Use a Bookkeeping System

Bookkeeping is different from accounting. It entails the recording of day-to-day transactions carried out in a business or organization. Accounting is a much broader concept that evaluates business performance and translates the data recorded by a bookkeeper into financial statements.

As a business owner, you need to know the bookkeeping method that is favorable to you. You can utilize the accrual or cash method. In the cash method, all expenses and revenues are recorded at the time you receive the income or pay for expenses. While the accrual method records revenues and expenses immediately the transaction occurs, revenues and expenses are recorded even if you have not received payment.

Record your Expenses and Revenues

If you want to keep good records and determine your business's progress, you need to learn how to track your income and expenses. It helps you track the progress of your business, make financial reports, prepare tax returns, and keep records of deductible expenses.

Set up a system for recording receipts and other important accounts. You should always pay attention to receipts like meals and entertainment, vehicle-related expenses, home office receipts, travel receipts, and receipts for gifts. Make sure these receipts are carefully recorded.

Set Up Sales Tax Procedures

As a business owner, you need to set up sales tax procedures. These days, sales tax has been added to most products. When selling to international clients, you might not need to charge sales tax. Set up your sales tax procedures accounting for your state or province.

Sales taxes vary by state and city. When you sell products, you need to charge your customers' sales tax. Before you charge sales tax in any province or state, you need to apply to charge sales tax and report the sales tax in the state you intend to do so.

Prepare for Some Expenses

It is normal for businesses to pay for unforeseen expenses. No matter how carefully you have created a balance sheet and maintain cash flow reports, you cannot predict some expenses. It is always nice to know you planned for unforeseen expenditures.

You can save an emergency fund in case there's an emergency. Keeping a separate emergency fund can help you pay unplanned expenses. Avoiding running into debt in your business will help you realize more profits.

Keep Vital Bookkeeping Records

As a business owner, you should keep important bookkeeping records. Keep documents like bills, sales receipts, tax returns, customer invoices, canceled checks, bank statements, 1099 forms, deposit slips, and payroll documentation.

Be sure and store bookkeeping records as a protected file on your computer and backed up, either on a hard drive or in the cloud. It is also a good idea to keep hard copies of these files in a safe place in your office.

CHAPTER 3

ACCRUAL METHOD VS. CASH BASIS METHOD

What are the Two Methods of Accounting?

One of the decisions you need to make before you start bookkeeping in your small business is choosing the right method for your business. The two major methods of bookkeeping are the accrual and the cash basis method.

Cash Basis Accounting

In the cash basis method, income is received and recorded immediately you render a service or sell a product. This method of accounting does not accept or record accounts payable or accounts receivable.

Most small businesses use the cash basis method because it has a simple approach. It is easy and simple to know if a transaction has been carried out, and you don't need to record payables or receivables. The cash basis method helps you to keep track of the amount of cash your business has at a particular period.

Pros:

Simple to operate: The cash basis method is a simple bookkeeping process that makes it easy to track your money. This accounting method is ideal for small businesses or organizations that do not deal with big inventory.

Convenient and reliable: This method of accounting is known for its reliability and convenience. With the cash basis accounting method, it is easy to keep track of your expenses and revenues.

Income taxes: If you are using this method, you are not required to pay taxes on any income that has not been received. For example, if you sold a product to a customer for $500 in November and you don't receive payment until March, you don't pay taxes until you have received the payment in March.

Cons:

- It does not track accounts payable or receivable.

- It gives an unclear financial picture.

- It does not abide by the Generally Accepted Accounting Principles.

Accrual Basis Accounting

In this method, expenses and revenues are recorded when they are incurred or generated, irrespective of when the payment is received. For instance, in the accrual basis method, revenue will be recorded when a transaction has been completely carried out and not when you receive payment. This method is more common than the cash basis method.

One disadvantage of using this method is that you cannot track the in-flow and out-flow of cash properly. This method of accounting is more complicated than cash basis accounting. In this method, you record transactions before you close your books for the month. This method keeps track of accounts receivable and accounts payable.

Pros:

Gives a clearer financial picture: This method gives a clearer financial picture of your business and shows a better idea of expenses and income incurred and earned during a financial period.

Conforms to GAAP: The accrual method of accounting abides by the Generally Accepted Accounting Principles, which is the main reason it is recommended for companies earning over $25 million annually.

Cons:

- It is more complex than the cash basis method.

- It is not ideal for small businesses.

- Comparing the two accounting methods

In the cash basis method, income is received and recorded immediately you render a service or sell a product. The cash basis method of accounting records transactions when cash is received. This method of accounting does not accept or record accounts payable or accounts receivable.

In the cash basis method, expenses and revenues are recorded when they are incurred or generated irrespective of when payment is received. In the accrual basis method, revenue will be recorded when a transaction has been completely carried out and not when you receive payment.

Which Method of Accounting is Suitable for Small Businesses?

According to the Internal Revenue Service, the accrual method is recommended for businesses that earn over $25 million on average. The Accrual method is suitable for corporations. The accrual method is used by corporations when reporting financial results or bookkeeping.

For small businesses, the cash basis method is recommended because of its simple nature. The choice of the accounting method to use is determined by the resources available, your business objectives, and the financial requirements of your business. However, the IRS advises that organizations must use the same method of accounting to report taxable income annually.

The cash basis method is ideal for small businesses that do not have inventory. If your business has a large inventory, the accrual method is ideal for you. For any business or organization that wants to change the methods of accounting, such a business is required to obtain approval from the Internal Revenue Service.

The accounting method you opt for influences the way you keep track of expenses and incomes on your financial statements. The Internal Revenue Service advises that businesses should utilize a consistent and effective accounting method. If you fail to be consistent with your accounting method, your tax returns will not be accepted by the IRS. Therefore, your business or organization may be penalized or fined.

Types of Bookkeeping Accounts

There are different accounts in bookkeeping. As a small business owner, you should know these accounts and understand how to record transactions in each of these accounts. You need to understand everything about your transactions. There are different types of accounts for small business bookkeeping. This section explains the different types of accounts in bookkeeping and how they are managed.

Sales

The sales account records all revenue generated from what you sell. All businesses generate sales by selling an item or product or by rendering services. Sales can be cash sales or credit sales. The difference between cash sales and credit sales is the time you receive payment. If you sell a product and receive payment immediately, it is called cash sales. When you sell on credit, you receive your payment in the future.

The sales account keeps track of all transactions related to sales. At the end of the month or year, the total sales are compared with the sales returns and allowances to get the net sales, which is recorded in the income statement.

Inventory

In financial accounting, goods yet to be sold are referred to as inventory. An organization's inventory refers to goods like raw materials, work-in-progress goods, and finished products that are ready to be sold. As a bookkeeper, you need to record inventory carefully.

Inventory is an asset meant for sale, or a product that is still in the process of production. The inventory account should be created and ensure you record the accurate inventory in this account.

Expenses

No matter how profitable your business is, you will need to spend on some things. You need to spend money to make more money. The salaries, wages, and rents you pay and the machines you repair are all examples of expenses. If you do not spend on labor or you fail to repair that book stapling machine, you cannot generate profit.

Expenses are categorized into two classes: recurring expenses and non-recurring expenses. Recurring expenses are expenses you incur regularly. These expenses are crucial for the smooth running of your business. Examples of recurring expenses are electricity, salaries, rent, travel, and insurance expenses. These expenses are incurred in every accounting period.

Non-recurring expenses are incurred unexpectedly. There are unforeseen expenses that are unlikely to happen during an accounting period. Non-recurring expenses are a one-time expense that is not expected to continue again because they do not occur regularly. Examples include losses incurred due to theft or fire, lawsuit payments, company's write-offs, etc.

Liabilities

Liabilities refer to the debts owed by your business. This involves loans you have gotten from lenders. It also includes payroll expenses and accounts payable. In a liability account, a company records all its obligations, customer deposits, debt, etc. Liabilities refer to the amount you owe your creditors.

You need to keep good records of all liabilities. Examples of liabilities are interest payable, customer deposits, wages payable, income taxes payable, accounts payable, salaries payable, and other accrued expenses.

Account Receivable

If you sell goods or services without collecting payment instantly, it is called receivables. One of the most important accounts you need to keep track of is the account receivable. Ensure you keep your accounts receivable up to date and accurate.

If you want to keep good account receivable balances, you need to create an account receivable report and ensure it is reviewed weekly. The account receivable report contains a list of customer invoices yet to be paid. To keep good records of the amount your customers owe you, you should review the account receivable report regularly.

Owner's Equity

The owner's equity refers to your investment in the business. The owner's equity account keeps records of the amount a business owner invests in the business. It is also known as net assets because it shows the amount of money an owner invested in the business, excluding the liabilities.

In small businesses bookkeeping, the owner's equity account is created to determine the amount of money the business owner invested in the business. You can calculate the owner's equity by summing up the current revenues, owner's capital account, and current contributions and then subtracting expenses and withdrawals.

CHAPTER 4

ACCOUNTING

Accounting and bookkeeping are related but are different concepts. Many people have studied accounting, and people that studied accounting are called accountants. Accounting is a very important aspect of businesses. Financial accounting helps business owners to determine the financial state of their businesses. This chapter discusses financial accounting and how it can be done in small businesses.

What is Accounting?

Accounting is a broad concept that entails the process of keeping track of financial transactions and summarizing financial transactions. The process of accounting is a vital aspect of businesses that reveals the performance of a business. Evaluating the performance of a business helps a business owner to develop strategies that will lead to a better running of the business.

55

Even if you do not own a business, accounting is required in our everyday lives. For instance, if you prepare a budget and account for all your expenses and income, then you are making an account of your finances. Small business make use of the accounting process to keep track of their financial details.

Accounting has existed for a long time, and it has helped so many businesses and organizations experience financial growth. Accounting helps you to assess the cash flow, expenses, income, liabilities, and assets of your organization. It is the backbone of a business, and without it, a business will crumble. A business needs financial accounting to thrive.

Accounting derives financial statements from bookkeeping, which helps a business make critical decisions. With the help of accounting, business owners know which strategies were helpful and what to do for the smooth running of their businesses. Accounting is defined as the art of recording, analyzing, measuring, and summarizing financial transactions of an organization.

Importance of Accounting in Small Businesses

Every business spends money and makes sales; accounting makes it easier to track these transactions. Below is the importance of accounting in a business:

Evaluates a Business' Performance

It is important you know the financial performance of your business because you have invested in this business. Accounting gives you a clear picture of what your business is like. Accounting reveals what you need to know about your business. As a business owner, you must know the performance of your business so that you can make good decisions that will improve your business.

The financial statements derived from bookkeeping reflect the financial position of your business. Accounting helps you to know how your business is fairing. As a business owner, it is your responsibility to know the financial health of your business. A business without proper accounting will fail.

Creates Future Projections

The process of accounting helps a business to make plans for the future. When you understand the financial position of your business, you will be able to make budgets and create projections for the future. Sometimes businesses spend on unforeseen projects; making plans for the future can help you solve some financial problems that may arise in the future.

Making future plans and projections for your business is based on past financial data. Business owners compare past and present financial data to make plans for the future. Proper accounting provides accurate and detailed financial statements to help you to create projections and make plans for the future.

Helps You Achieve Your Goal

Proper accounting helps you accomplish your objectives. If your objective is to sell more or acquire more assets, you can achieve this goal by proper accounting. Accounting gives you a clear picture of the financial standing of your business, which will help you plan for the future.

Ensures Statutory Compliance

The law and regulations guiding businesses vary from one state to another. Proper accounting helps you to abide by these laws. For instance, according to the IRS, a business should use the accrual basis of accounting method when they earn over $25 million monthly.

Proper accounting addresses liabilities like VAT, pension funds, income tax, and sales tax properly. Accounting helps your business comply with the laws and regulations related to business in your state.

Basic Accounting Terminology

As a business owner, you should understand some commonly used accounting terms.

Assets

Assets refer to any resources or items owned by your business. Assets often appear on your balance sheet. Examples of assets are inventory, machinery, accounts receivable, a loan given to an employee, etc.

Liabilities

Liabilities refer to the amount owed by a business or organization. Examples of liabilities are tax payable, account payable, equipment loans, etc. Anything your business owes other entities is known as a liability.

Debits

Debits are accounting terms that refer to entries in your ledger. Debits record transactions on the left column of an account. Debits are often balanced by credits when closing your books. Expenses are always debited in the general ledger.

Credits

Credits are the opposite of debits. Credits record transactions at the right column of an account. For each debit entry, there must be a credit entry and vice versa. A credit entry increases an equity account or decreases an expense or asset account.

Income Statement

Income statement states the expense incurred and the income generated from business operations during a financial period. The income statement is a vital financial statement that reveals the financial performance of a business over a given period. It reveals the amount of profit generated in a business or the loss incurred.

The General Ledger

The general ledger records all financial transactions of a business or organization. It consists of the debit and credit column. It records assets, liabilities, income, profits, expenses, and losses.

Expenditure

It is normal for businesses to spend money. Expenditure is anything you spend money on. When your expenditures become greater than your income, then you have incurred a loss. Any cost incurred to get a particular item or to generate revenue is regarded as an expenditure.

Balance Sheet

A balance sheet in financial accounting refers to a financial statement that reports the financial position of a business at a particular time. The balance sheet reports the assets, equity, and liabilities of a business. The balance sheet is one of the most important financial reports in accounting.

Owner's Equity

The owner's equity refers to the amount you own in your business. The owner's equity is the investment of the owner in the business subtracted by the owner's withdrawals from the business with the addition of the net income. As a business owner, you have claims to the equity.

Fixed Costs

Fixed costs are costs that do not change regardless of the business activities. These costs are incurred frequently, and they do not fluctuate with sales. Examples of fixed costs are utility bills, rent, salaries, insurance, property taxes, interest expense, etc. These costs are sometimes called general & administrative or overhead expenses.

Variable Costs

This type of cost is the opposite of fixed costs. These costs change from time to time, based on the financial position of a business. Variable costs are not static; they fluctuate. The level of output in a business or organization determines these costs. Examples of fixed costs include production supply, commissions, freight out, etc.

Capital

Capital in accounting refers to the amount of money or resources used to start up a business. Examples of capital are tangible equipment, buildings, funds in deposit accounts, production equipment, etc. Capital can also be calculated by the deduction of a business liability from its assets.

Return Inwards

Return inwards are goods returned by a customer after they have been sold. Return inwards are recorded in a trading account. Return inwards are always debited in the general ledger.

Return Outwards

Return outwards, also known purchase returns, are goods returned by an organization after they have been purchased. These goods can be returned based on some damage or any other reason.

Branches of Accounting

Accounting is a broad field having several branches. This section explains the different branches of accounting.

Management Accounting

Management accounting is a subfield of accounting that is concerned with financial information that is needed for management. Management accounting utilizes financial data for decision-making purposes. This information is not published; it is used to evaluate the performance of a business, determine the profitability of a business, and to assist in making decisions.

The users of this accounting information are the managers. The accounting information is organized in a way that makes it simple for managers to understand and analyze. This subfield of accounting analyzes financial operations and costs to make financial statements, records, or reports.

Financial Accounting

Financial accounting is one of the branches of accounting that deals with how financial reports are prepared. This branch of accounting involves the interpretation of the financial statements of an organization. It provides users with the necessary financial information. Financial accounting records and summarizes financial transactions of an organization.

Financial accounting abides by the Generally Accepted Accounting Principles. The Generally Accepted Accounting Principles are the rules guiding the preparation of financial reports. They ensure that financial reports are reliable and useful. Several accounting techniques like ledgers, journals, trial balance, etc. are used to keep financial records.

Cost Accounting

Cost accounting is a branch of accounting that records, analyzes, and interprets the cost incurred on a service or product in business. It involves the process of recording, classifying, and determining the costs of goods and services. Cost accounting helps to calculate the cost of every service and product.

Cost accounting involves three major areas: cost reduction, cost control, and cost ascertainment. Cost accounting helps a business to determine the price of a service or product, make better decisions, calculate the break-even point, and prevent wastage. Cost accounting is useful in creating budgets and make plans for an organization.

Auditing

Auditing is a branch of accounting that deals with the examination of the financial statements or reports of an organization to determine its accuracy. Auditing refers to the process of inspecting, reviewing, verifying, and evaluating the financial records of an organization. The person who does this job is regarded as an auditor.

Auditing ensures that the financial records of an organization comply with the rules and regulations guiding accounting. According to accounting laws, all public companies should audit their financial statements. External auditors are not part of the organization's staff; they keep a check on the financial records and provide a statement on these records. Internal auditors are part of the organization; they are employed by the organization to keep a check on financial records.

Tax Accounting

Tax accounting is a branch of accounting that is concerned with taxes. The sole purpose of tax accounting is to keep a check on the funds of a company and ensures that a company complies with tax regulations. The rules and regulations guiding tax accounting are the Internal Revenue Code. Businesses and organizations must adhere to the rules and regulations of the IRC when calculating their tax returns.

Tax accounting is concerned with how tax payments and returns are made. The type of tax returns you submit is based on the type of business you operate. A tax accountant can calculate the amount of tax you are required to pay.

There are other branches of accounting, like government accounting, forensic accounting, fund accounting, and fiduciary accounting. All these branches of accounting are concerned with specializing in their field. Accounting is very crucial in businesses, organizations, and the government system.

CHAPTER 5

HOW TO RECORD TRANSACTIONS

Accounting and bookkeeping exist because business transactions exist. Without any business transaction, there is no need for bookkeeping and accounting. Bookkeeping keeps up-to-date and well-detailed records of business transactions. In every organization or business, financial or business transactions exist. This chapter explains what a business transaction is, how to record business transactions, the features of a business transaction, accounting equations, and the classification of a business transaction.

What is a Business Transaction?

Business transaction describes activities and events of a monetary business that has a financial effect on a business. A business transaction is also known as a financial transaction. For instance, you have a business, and you purchase raw materials that are needed for the production of your goods. If you purchase these raw materials and you paid $1000 cash for it, it is a financial activity that affects your business financially.

Bookkeeping and accounting systems only record activities that have a financial impact on the business. The salary you pay to your employees, the goods you purchase, the products you sell to your customers, and the rent you pay are good examples of financial transactions because they all involve money.

Some events do not have a monetary value. These kinds of events cannot be recorded as financial or business transactions. Since business transactions have to deal with money, any other type of event that does not involve money is not regarded as a financial transaction. For example, if a worker volunteers to teach his colleagues some accounting skills without demanding payment, this would not involve a financial transaction. Although this activity has a positive impact on the company, it cannot be classified as a business transaction.

An accountant or a bookkeeper keeps track of the financial transaction by creating a journal entry. The accountant or bookkeeper ensures that business transactions are authorized and supported by some documents before putting it in the journal. Some business transactions are recorded in the sales or purchases journal before posting them to the general ledger, while some transactions are directly recorded in the general ledger.

Features of a Business Transaction

A business transaction is not just recorded; it must have some features that will make it classified and recorded as a business transaction. We need to know that there are financial and non-financial transactions. Therefore, one has to be careful when recording financial transactions. Before you classify and record a transaction as a business transaction, you need to look for the following features or characteristics:

It Must be a Monetary Activity

A transaction that involves money is said to be a business transaction. A business transaction must have a monetary value. For instance, William Productions provides event management services for the sum of $5,000. Such a transaction is a business transaction for William Productions because it involves money.

It Must Involve the Business Entity

A transaction is regarded as a financial if it involves the business entity and affects the business's financial position. If Mr. William, the CEO of William

Productions, purchases a car with his own money for his use, such a transaction will not be recorded in the company's account because the transaction does not involve the business.

If Mr. William invests $5,000 into the business, such a transaction will be recorded in the company's account because it involves the business entity and also affects the business's financial position.

It Must have a Dual Impact on the Accounting Elements

A transaction is recorded as a financial transaction when it has a dual effect. This means for each debit entry, there must be a credit entry and vice versa. This is the principle of double-entry accounting.

For instance, William productions bought some drapes for decoration for $3,500. The drapes purchased increased the company's assets. The company gave out some amount of money to get drapes; therefore, there is a decrease in the company's cash. The company's asset account is debited, while the cash account is credited.

It Must have the Support of a Source Document

A financial transaction has to be supported by a source document. A source document contains the original details of a business transaction. A source document records the vital details of a transaction. It makes records of the date, the amount paid, and the names of the entities involved in the transaction.

Source documents are crucial to internal auditors because they are used as a source of evidence. A source document is used as a piece of evidence by a business organization when dealing with their clients. Source documents include checks, invoices, bank statements, sales receipts, payroll reports, and purchase orders.

Classification of Business Transactions

Business transactions are classified into cash and credit transactions and internal and external transactions.

Cash Transaction

A business transaction is classified as a cash transaction if payment is received in cash immediately. In cash transactions, payment can be made with a check or credit card. As long as the payment is made at the time of business transactions, it is a cash transaction.

What differentiates a cash transaction from a credit transaction is the time of payment. Cash sales, purchase of goods by cash, and cash transactions are examples of cash transactions.

Credit Transaction

A credit transaction is a type of transaction in which payment is made at a future date. For instance, if you sell a product to a customer and expect payment at a future date, such a transaction is called a credit transaction.

When credit transaction occurs, the payment is not made at the time the business transactions takes place, which means cash is paid or received at a future time. Most goods are purchased and sold on credit.

Internal Transaction

Internal transactions are transactions made with no external entities involved. It is a transaction in which no outsider is involved. It is a business transaction that is made within the same organization. Provision of services and goods to a department of the same organization and calculating and recording depreciation are good examples of internal transactions.

External Transaction

This refers to a transaction that involves external parties. This kind of transaction occurs between organizations and involves a transaction between a business and another entity. The sale or purchase of goods from another party, purchase of goods from a supplier, and payment of salary are examples of external transactions. The majority of the business transactions recorded are external transactions.

The Rules for Identifying a Cash and Credit Transaction

Sometimes, business owners become confused in determining the type of transaction. There are rules to determine if a transaction is a credit or cash. These rules are explained below.

A transaction is classified as cash if the name of the buyer or seller is not mentioned in the transaction. For instance, purchased goods for $300.

A transaction is recorded as a cash transaction if 'cash' is involved. For example, purchasing goods for $100 from Mr. Edwards.

If "on credit" is mentioned in a transaction, such a transaction is classified as a credit transaction.

If the buyer's or seller's name is mentioned in the transaction. For instance, they purchased goods for $1000 from Mr. Edwards.

All business transactions must have a financial impact on a business. Business transactions affect the asset, owner's equity, revenues, liabilities, and expenses of a business. With these rules, business owners, accountants, and bookkeepers can easily determine if a business transaction is a cash or credit.

Accounting Equations

The accounting equation is the fundamental of accounting and a crucial element of the balance sheet. The accounting equation shows the balance sheet's structure. In the accounting equation, assets are derived by the sum of liabilities and shareholder's equity. Accountants and bookkeepers should always apply the accounting equation when making journal entries.

You can also derive the shareholder's equity by subtracting liabilities from assets, i.e., Shareholder's equity = Assets - Liabilities. The accounting equation must balance. The accounting equation reveals the economic impacts of financial transactions in a business. Liabilities can also be derived by subtracting equity from assets. It reveals how economic activities affect the balance sheet.

The expanded accounting equation reveals the interaction between your balance sheet and income statement. The expanded accounting equation is calculated by Assets = Liabilities + Income + Owner's Equity − Expenses − Draws. Income increases the owner's equity; expenses reduce the owner's equity, and the Owner's draw reduces the owner's equity.

For instance, if Just Rite Enterprise decides to buy a new asset, such as a vehicle that costs $5000, the company can purchase the vehicle by paying with cash (company's assets), with a liability (a loan) or with owner's equity (funds). If the purchase is carried out by using liability, the $ 5,000 can be paid using cash (assets).

The Importance of the Accounting Equation

The accounting equation is very important in accounting and bookkeeping. It shows the interactions that exist among the owner's equity, liabilities, and assets. It is the fundamental of the double-entry system.

Preparation of Financial Reports

The accounting equation is very vital when preparing financial reports. It is used to create a financial report like the balance sheet. The balance sheet is a yearly report that can be prepared quarterly and derived from the accounting equations.

It is the Basis of the Double-Entry System

The accounting equation is the basis of the double-entry system in accounting. It ensures that the books of a company are balanced.

Reveals the Financial Position of a Business

The accounting equation provides the financial performance of your business. If you want to make a financial report of your business, you will need to calculate the accounting equation. The accounting equation reveals the interaction between your income statements and the balance sheet.

Shows the Worth of a Company

Another importance of the accounting equation is that it shows the financial worth of a company. The accounting equation reveals how much your business has in the bank. It helps you to evaluate the value of investments in a business. It helps you to know the net worth of your business. It also helps investors to decide on investing in a company.

Helps to Make Critical Decisions

As a business owner, the accounting equation helps you to make critical decisions in your business. With this equation, you can know if you can go ahead with purchasing an asset or not. It will also reveal if your business is financially capable of paying off debts with the existing assets or by taking more loans.

How Business Transactions are Analyzed

Analysis of business transaction studies how the financial performance of businesses changes due to financial transactions. Different financial transactions affect a business's financial position. Business transactions change the five main elements of accounting, which include capital, income, expenses, assets, and liabilities.

The accounting principle states that every business transaction must have a two-fold effect on a business. For instance, Mrs. Palmer, the CEO of Palmer's Enterprises, buys equipment worth $16,000. This business transaction has a two-fold effect. The equipment, which is the company's asset, will increase by $16,000, and the company's cash, which is also an asset, will decrease by $16,000. Therefore, these changes are reflected in the company's assets.

If the equipment was bought on credit from another organization, there will be two changes. The equipment will increase by $16,000, and the company's liability will increase by $16,000.

How to Record Business Transactions

When analyzing and recording a business transaction, there are certain steps you need to take, these steps are:

Determining the accounts involved: For every business transaction that occurs, there are two or more accounts involved. The first step in analyzing a business transaction is determining the accounts that are involved.

Identifying the nature of the accounts: This is the second procedure you follow when analyzing a business transaction. You need to know if the transaction is an asset account or a capital account.

Determining the impacts based on the decrease and increase: You need to identify the account that is decreasing and the one that is increasing - two accounts can increase at the same time.

Apply the credit and debit rule: This is the last procedure you take when analyzing business transactions. In this procedure, you need to determine the account that needs to be debited and credited.

Journal Entries

A journal is a financial record that keeps track of transactions. Examples of the journal include purchases journal, sales journal, cash disbursements journal, and cash receipts journal. Some transactions are recorded in a journal before they are recorded in the general ledger. The most important journal is the general journal. The general journal records every business transaction carried out in a business.

The sales journal records all sales made on credit or a business's inventory. The return inward journal records goods that were sold but returned by customers. The first place a transaction is recorded is the journal. The general ledger is prepared from the entries made in the journal.

How to Perform Accounting Journal Entries

Before preparing a journal, you need to record the financial details of your transactions. You can get the financial details of your transactions from purchase orders, cash register tapes, invoices, and other sources. Once the transaction has been analyzed, you can record the financial data in the journal. Every transaction recorded in the journal is called a journal entry.

The double-entry system is used when recording transactions in the journal. For every entry, there must be a debit and credit column. For instance, if Mr. A buys machinery with cash, the accounts affected are the asset account and the cash account. The cash account will increase while the asset account will increase.

The single-entry system can also be used for recording transactions in the journal, but this system is rarely used.

In this system, only a single account exists for every entry made in the journal. While balancing the journal, make sure the credits and the debit balance well.

The Difference Between a General Ledger a Journal

Financial transactions are recorded in the general ledger and journal. The journal is a document where transactions are recorded first before they are entered in the ledger. The general ledger summarizes financial information.

The journal keeps a record of all financial transactions carried out in business while the ledger records the financial details used for preparing financial statements. The journal, which is always referred to as a document of original entry, is used for making ledger while the ledger is used for preparing final accounts and trial balance.

Entries recorded in the journal are done in chronological order, while transactions are posted in the general ledger by using the double-entry system. You do not need to balance the journal, but the general ledger needs to be balanced.

Bookkeepers and accountants make use of the general ledger to keep track of all relevant accounts. The general ledger has the debit and the credit side, and it uses the T format when recording transactions.

Debits/Credits

In the accounting world, the debit side is the left side of an account, while the credit side is the right side of an account. For every business transaction, there must be credit as well as a debit entry. The principle of double-entry reveals that for each debit entry, a credit entry must be available and vice versa.

When recording a business transaction, you need to determine the two accounts involved. After you have done that, you need to know the accounts that will be debited and the one to be credited. Your journal entries are prepared so that the debit side is at the left and credit side on the right.

In the journal entry, the debit side records an increase in assets and any decrease in the owner's equity and liabilities. For example, if a company purchases a vehicle, the company's assets account will be debited while the cash account is credited since the company's cash is decreasing.

The debit total and the credit total must balance according to the principles of the double-entry system. When the two entries are well balanced, it shows that there are no errors in the transactions recorded. For instance, if a company purchases office supplies with $200 cash, there are two accounts involved, the cash account and the office supplies account. $200 is credited in the cash account, while $500 is debited in the office supplies account.

Let us take a look at the following examples:

Step 1

If Mr. Andrews uses $300,000 to start his business.

Transaction analysis:

Two changes have occurred because of this financial transaction;

1. The owner's equity has increased by $300,000.

2. Cash (an asset) has increased by $300,000.

Step 2

If he deposits $80,000 in the bank

Transaction Analysis:

This transaction has resulted in two changes

1. The cash balance (an asset) will decrease by $80,000

2. The bank balance (an asset) will increase by $80,000

Step 3

If he takes a loan of $50,000 from Mr. Whitney at 10% per annum.

Transaction Analysis:

1. The cash balance increases by $50,000.

2. The liability increases by $50,000.

Step 4

If he buys furniture for $50,000 by cash.

Transaction Analysis:

The two changes that occurred due to this transaction are:

1. The asset has increased by $50,000

2. The cash balance has decreased by $50,000

Step 5

If he buys goods from Mr. Walker for $70,000 and paid with cash $50,000

Transaction analysis:

Three changes have occurred due to this transaction; they are:

1. Purchases (goods) have increased by $70,000

2. Cash balance has decreased by $50,000

3. Liability has increased by $20,000

CHAPTER 6

ESTABLISHING A SYSTEM

In the old days, business owners, accountants, and bookkeepers recorded transactions using the paper process. They used paper and pencil to make lots of columns, record transactions, and prepare financial statements. In today's world, the story has taken another dimension because several accounting applications have been developed to record transactions.

Business owners can decide to perform the bookkeeping or accounting tasks themselves. Some accounting software can be used to record transactions and perform bookkeeping tasks. Even small business owners can find suitable accounting software for their businesses. There are lots of benefits business owners get from using accounting software.

This chapter discusses the functions and benefits of accounting software, the types of accounting software, how to choose the right accounting software for your business, and how much it costs to get accounting software.

Excel – Spreadsheets

The Microsoft Excel spreadsheet is one of the applications designed to perform accounting tasks. Excel helps to perform tasks like preparation of financial statements, preparation of balance sheets, performing some calculations, etc. Excel spreadsheets can be used to keep track of business transactions. With these spreadsheets, accountants can prepare some accounts which can be stored in the computer and used for decision making.

Excel spreadsheets are commonly used by accountants. These spreadsheets help users organize and summarize data in an easy to use format. Regardless of the size of your business, Microsoft Excel spreadsheets can be used to perform accounting tasks. As a small business owner, Excel helps you to tabulate, organize, calculate, summarize, and store accounting data.

In Excel, you can use the cash basis or the accrual basis method of accounting. When using the accrual method, you have to set up different accounts. When adopting the double-entry principle, you have to make use of the accounting equation.

If you prefer the cash basis method, you need to prepare a new worksheet and put column headers for the transaction description, date, and transaction number. Accountants have long used Microsoft Excel, and it has proved to be a useful and reliable application.

Accounting Software - QuickBooks

What is Accounting Software?

Accounting software is an application used by accountants to keep track of the flow of cash for external and internal review. It is a financial tool that helps a business to evaluate its financial performance. Accounting software abides by the laws guiding accounting. Accounting software helps to reduce mistakes that can be made using a pencil and paper.

Accounting software helps you to get sales projections for the next quarter, evaluate the financial performance of your business, and determine the items you need in your business. Accounting software offers a wide variety of benefits for users. If you want to run a successful business, you need to consider using effective accounting software.

Accounting software should abide by the accounting rules and regulations of your state or country. For instance, if you are in the United Kingdom, the choice of your accounting software should comply with Making Tax Digital. In the United States, accounting software should comply with the Sweeping Tax Cuts and Jobs Act.

Examples of Accounting Software

FreeAgent

FreeAgent is an accounting software that helps bookkeepers, accountants, and business owners to manage their transactions. This software carries out the management of invoices, payroll, expenses, and other accounting activities. FreeAgent makes use of the double-entry method of accounting, which makes it user-friendly.

FreshBooks

FreshBooks is an effective accounting applications you can use to perform your accounting and bookkeeping tasks. Over 5 million organizations around the globe use this software. This software is suitable for small businesses that want to operate following the regulations and standards of their state or country. FreshBooks is a mobile-friendly software that is very easy to operate.

Zoho Books

Zoho Books is a powerful online software that offers a wide variety of features that help small businesses to manage cash flow in their business. Purchase and sale order management, management of expenditure, invoicing, time tracking, contact management, and inventory management are some of the features offered by this accounting software.

Zoho Books is a high-quality application that automates payment reminders, bank statements, and invoices. It provides upgrades on some of its features, such as custom domains and invoice templates.

Tipalti

This accounting software is created to make the process of account payable easier. Some features it offers include automation of invoice, calculation of tax, regulatory compliance management, supplier management, and payment remittance. Tipalti ensures that the financial data of your business is processed in an easy to understand language.

With this software, issues like non-compliance, late payments, and over-tasking the accountant are prevented. Tipalti features ERP systems, payment reconciliation, and AP. This software makes global mass payments very simple. With Tipalti, you can make use of 120 currency options and depend on six different methods of payment like debit card, PayPal, local bank transfer, and wire.

Sage Business Cloud Accounting

For small business owners that need effective accounting software, Sage business cloud accounting has got you covered. It provides features that meet the requirement of small business accounting. For small business owners, you can utilize the entry-level accounting solution with Sage.

It provides features like minimizing spreadsheets, managing finances, and reducing paperwork. This software makes business payroll simple and easy to handle, manages cash flow, and automates financial processes.

Tradogram

This software is specifically developed to ensure the smooth running of the purchasing process of your business. The software features built-in tools that help in tracking expenses, managing suppliers, and controlling costs. Tradogram offers some accounting tools for generating contracts, invoices, Pos, and other documents.

Xero

Xero helps small business owners and financial managers to have access to financial information on any device. This application is mobile-friendly. It helps small business owners to keep track of account receivables, expenditures, account payables, revenues, and wages. With Xero, you can reconcile your bank transactions.

Types of Accounting Software

There are different kinds of accounting software you can use for your small business. When choosing accounting software, it should be based on the type and nature of your business. There are four major categories of accounting software. The four categories are:

Payroll Management Systems

If you want to take charge of your account receivables and account payables, you should consider opting for the payroll management system. These applications were designed to carry out different business tasks, such as employees' salaries calculation, pay slips and tax forms, cutting deductions, etc. This category of accounting software will keep your financial transactions secure and help you make detailed financial reports. Examples of payroll management systems include AccountEdge, Xero, and Zenefits.

Time and Expense Management Systems

Applications that belong to this category include Zoho Expense, FreshBooks, and Expensify. These applications are specifically developed to speed up billing cycles. They make the payment process faster and help detect slow and inefficient payment processes. The greatest benefit these systems offer is the production of detailed graphs on how resources and time can be managed within a company.

Billing and Invoicing Systems

Zoho Books, FreshBooks, and Zoho Invoice are examples of applications that belong to this category. These applications help businesses to complete basic and daily tasks. These tasks include informing clients about due payments and check writing. These systems feature invoicing and billing tools that help to prepare a financial event for validation and authorization.

Enterprise Resource Planning Systems

This category of accounting software is important. It includes the systems required for inventory management, cost control, finance, material purchasing, human resource, finance, product planning, and accounting. Newly designed ERP solutions provide modules for Customer relations Management and business intelligence. Applications like Odoo, Intact, and Brightpearl belong to this category.

Functions of Accounting Software

Billing and invoicing: Some accounting applications are specifically designed for carrying out the tasks of invoicing and billing. When you need to know who owes you money, the amount, and the due date for payment, accounting software has got you covered. Most accounting systems enable you to print invoices and send them to your customers through email. Your accounting system will provide information as regards the name, account numbers, and address of the customer.

These accounting systems also provide automatic invoicing. Automatic invoicing in accounting systems ensure that your income is not delayed, even if you have forgotten to send an invoice. The accounting software reminds your customers when to pay their bills.

Payroll management: Accounting software offers a wide variety of payroll features that will help you to calculate the employee payments and also print checks quickly. In some accounting systems, payroll modules are very effective. They are in control of all aspects of payroll.

Accounting software helps to handle various pay schedules having various kinds of compensation in your company. Some workers are paid daily, weekly, or monthly; the accounting software will help you to handle these payments.

Forecasting and budgeting: Accounting software helps businesses to plan and make a budget. Most accounting applications provide details about the financial performance of a business by calculating and interpreting the company's financial data. With effective accounting software, small businesses and companies can make a budget for the future.

With the provision of necessary financial details, companies can make critical decisions as regards their finances. Businesses can also make feasible goals.

Accounting: Accounting software performs accounting tasks. An effective accounting system should consist of features like accounts payable, account receivables, general ledgers, etc. The primary component of every accounting system is accounting.

Inventory management: An accounting application that features inventory and stock controls can help you to know what you have in stock and what you need to purchase. Accounting software helps you track and manage your inventory, know the type of stocks you need to get and determine stock locations.

Banking: Accounting software helps you to make payments directly from your bank and as well enable you to import information directly from the bank into the accounting system. If your business uses more than one bank account, you should get an accounting system that will help you reconcile your accounts.

Accounting software also helps you to make payments with the use of checks. Some systems offer features that enable you to process and print your checks. They also provide features like bank deposits preparation, check to handle, and check to void.

Time management: This is an important function performed by accounting systems. Most businesses and companies need to track the time spent on accomplishing specific tasks. Time modules offered by accounting systems are very helpful in tracking the time an employee spent in accomplishing a task. This ensures you calculate the accurate payroll in your business.

Shipping: Some accounting systems save you the stress and money to invest in shipment software. As a business owner that often sends goods using a courier service, you can consider opting for accounting systems that make the process of shipping goods easier.

With this accounting system, you can easily track what you have shipped and calculate delivery times accurately.

Some applications help you to know how distance and weight vary; this will help you calculate accurate shipping costs.

Why You Should Use Accounting Software

There are several benefits you enjoy when you use accounting software. Accounting software is a tool used by most accountants and bookkeepers to perform accounting and bookkeeping tasks. These applications can make the tax returns calculation easy and also comply with specific requirements in your state or country. You should use accounting software for the following reasons:

It is easy to use: It provides information that can be understood by an audience who has little or no experience in accounting. With accounting software, a business owner can perform all accounting tasks without hiring an external party to perform the tasks.

It saves money: With effective accounting software, you do not need to hire an external expert to help you perform your accounting tasks. Accounting software helps you perform calculations and administrative tasks and as well manage your revenue. Accounting applications reduce the cost of printing documents.

It complies with tax rules: This is one of the benefits of using accounting software. Most accounting applications abide by tax rules and regulations. Immediately they are installed; they carry out their accounting tasks with compliance to the tax rules.

It helps to improve performance: If a business owner needs to improve the performance of her business, she should consider using accounting software. Accounting software collects, organizes, and summarizes the crucial part of the accounting data available. With the information provided by accounting software, you can evaluate your business's performance and make decisions that will improve your business.

It provides security: A company's financial data is vital information that needs to be kept securely. This data should not fall into the wrong hands. Accounting software ensures the security of your financial data. In most cases, they always come with a password.

It is transparent: Accounting applications provide automating calculations. One of the benefits of using accounting software is that it prevents costly errors. Previously, lots of errors were made when using the paper and pencil method. Errors can mislead a business and negatively affect business performance.

Factors to Consider When Choosing Accounting Software for Your Small Business

Accounting software offers lots of benefits for users. It is easier, faster, more efficient, and better than the pencil and paper method. As a small business owner, your top priority is the financial performance of your business and how to improve it.

You need an accounting system that will help you perform and accomplish your accounting tasks as well as give you a clear picture of the financial performance of your business. One of the most critical decisions you will make as a business owner is choosing the right accounting software for your business. Each software offers different features and several pricing plans you can opt for. You need to consider some factors before choosing an accounting system; these factors are discussed below:

Ease of use: You need to consider how easy and simple the accounting software you are opting for is. The information should be well-arranged, and calculations should be made simple.

Mobile-ready: This is an important factor you should take into consideration. These days, most accounting systems offer iOS and Android applications for users.

The mobile apps also offer the same features as the desktop versions.

Cost: The price of accounting software varies; this depends on the number of features and the kinds of plans it offers. Some companies provide users with a free version of their accounting applications. You should opt for an accounting system that meets your budget.

Security: Accounting software keeps the vital information of a business; therefore, you need to consider the security mechanism of your preferred software.

Multi-user support: You need accounting software that will support several small businesses with one account. This should be an important factor for business owners with multiple businesses. If your software features multi-user support, it saves you the cost of establishing separate accounts for every entity.

CHAPTER 7

GENERAL LEDGER

The Charts of Accounts, general ledger, and Journal are vital accounts in bookkeeping. In the double-entry bookkeeping system, business transactions are recorded in the journal and general ledger. This chapter explains the general ledger, journal, and trial balance. It discusses how transactions are recorded in these three books.

General Ledger: What Does This Mean?

The general ledger is an important book in accounting that utilizes the double-entry system. In the traditional sense, accountants and bookkeepers record business transactions in the general ledger by utilizing the double-entry system of accounting. The advancement in technology has made the preparation of ledger easier. There are excel sheets and accounting software that can help you prepare ledgers.

Most financial reports are derived from the ledger. The general ledger records and summarizes all the business transactions that occur in an organization. This accounting document ensures that all entries have a debit and credit record. An entry in an account must have an opposite entry in another. The general ledger operates per the double-entry principle, which states that "for each credit entry, there must be a debit entry and vice versa."

Why a General Ledger is Important

The general ledger is very important in accounting. Small business owners can prepare the general ledger to record financial transactions carried out in their businesses. Although the general ledger is not compulsory, you can decide not to use it based on the nature of your business. The general ledger is important because it does the following:

- It gives a clear picture of your business at any time. For instance, a cash ledger will show the cash in hand at a particular time.

- It makes the process of bank reconciliation faster because all financial transactions related to a bank account are recorded in one place.

- It gives reports of expenses and revenues which help you know what to spend on.

- Auditors require it because it reflects the transactions carried out in your business.

- It helps you to detect any fraudulent practices in your business.

- With the general ledger, filing tax returns is easier since all your revenue and expenses are recorded in one place.

Posting Transactions to Separate Ledger Account

A general ledger contains separate accounts like purchases, cash, sales, etc. Journal entries are posted in the ledger account. When posting entries in the general ledger, you need to open a separate account for every account, and transactions from the journal are transferred to each ledger account.

If you debit any account in the journal, you will also debit it in the ledger account. All transactions in the journal entry must be recorded in the ledger account. As a business owner, you need to post your transactions in the general ledger.

For instance, if a company sold goods worth $3,000 for cash, there are two separate accounts in this business transaction. The separate accounts opened in the general ledger are cash account and sales account. The cash account is debited, while the sales account is credited. The cash account is receiving some cash, while the sales account will decrease by $3,000.

The general ledger includes accounts like cash, accounts payable, capital stock, notes payable, office equipment, etc. Entries in the journal are recorded in the general ledger using the double-entry system. The ledger accounts records transactions associated with a particular account. For instance, sales are recorded in the sales account, purchases are recorded in the purchases account, and account receivable is recorded in the account receivable account, and so on.

The Charts of Account

The Charts of Accounts keeps all the accounts prepared for recording a financial transaction. It is a document that lists all the accounts required in the general ledger of a business. Several business transactions are carried out daily in a company. A Chart of Accounts consists of equity, assets, income, expenditure, and liabilities.

The Chart of Accounts provides all the business transactions carried out in a company during an accounting period. It describes the name of every account that is listed and the identification number of each account. The chart of accounts includes the income statement accounts and balance sheet accounts.

The Chart of Accounts is a vital financial aspect of a business because it is specifically designed to record all the liability, revenue, assets, equity, and expenses of the organization. A company can design its chart of accounts based on the type of business it is operating. Chart of accounts is a useful source of financial information for external parties that need to know about an organization.

The chart of account provides the necessary information about a company and its daily operations. A small business needs to set up its CoA when starting a business. The chart of accounts is set up based on the nature or type of business operated.

How to Set Up the Chart of Accounts

A Chart of Accounts is created based on the nature of the business. For instance, business rendering catering services will create certain accounts that are related to the catering business. The catering business can include a transport expense account, which might not be common in all businesses. This catering business might exclude the inventory account since the business renders services.

Identification codes are included in the CoA, and these codes help you to identify some accounts easily. Identification codes enable you to record transactions easily. A three-digit number is often used in small businesses, while a four-digit number is often used in larger businesses. You need to ensure that the numbering follows a pattern to make work easier for the management.

The number of accounts in the CoA depends on the size of the organization - larger businesses with several divisions will typically have more accounts than the smaller businesses. The Chart of Accounts must be prepared according to the Financial Accounting Standards Board and Generally Accepted Accounting Principles.

The Categories of Chart of Accounts

The Chart of Account is categorized into two financial statements - the balance sheet and the income statement.

Balance Sheet Accounts

The balance sheet is a financial statement that consists of liability accounts, asset accounts, and the owner's equity account.

Asset accounts

The asset account contains the records of a company's assets. Assets are classified as current assets and fixed assets, tangible or intangible assets. Examples of a company's assets are cash in hand, inventory assets, savings account, and prepaid insurance.

Liability accounts

The liability account is the record of the debts owed by a company. Examples of liabilities include invoice payable, salary payable, account payable, etc. Just like the asset account, in the liability accounts, current liabilities come before long-term liabilities.

Owner's equity accounts

The owner's equity account reflects the net worth of business after liabilities have been subtracted from the company's assets. The owner's equity reveals the net worth of businesses to shareholders. Examples of transactions recorded in this account include retained profits, common stock, and preferred stocks.

The Income Statement

The income statement is one of the most important financial reports of a company. This statement reflects the profit generated and the loss incurred in a business during an accounting period. The statement records all income and subtracts all expenses from the income. By doing this, the profit or loss of a company is determined. The purpose of this statement is to quickly show investors whether the business made money or lost money.

The Importance of the Chart of Accounts

- It keeps records of all business transactions.

- It reflects the financial position of a business and provides a clear picture of your business.

- It can be designed based on the nature of the business

- It helps to prepare the financial reports of a company.

- It is easy to control costs because it records all accounts separately.

- It helps your business adhere to financial reporting principles.

The Chart of Accounts, journal, and general ledger are very vital in accounting. Small business owners should use these accounts when recording transactions as they provide lots of benefits for business owners. If you want to run a successful business, you should consider using these financial documents since they reflect the financial position of a business.

CHAPTER 8

PREPARING TRIAL BALANCE FOR SMALL BUSINESSES

After the general ledger has been prepared, you must prepare a trial balance for your small business. This chapter discusses the usefulness of trial balance and how you can prepare a trial balance for your small business.

As a small business owner, you may not like performing bookkeeping and accounting tasks, but you need to perform these tasks to run a successful business. You need to prepare the trial balance to ensure that your accounts are correctly recorded. The trial balance will help you detect some mistakes in your double-entry books.

The Meaning of a Trial Balance

A trial balance is a financial report in which the balances of the general ledger of a business are recorded at a particular point in time. The accounts recorded in trial balance are associated with the major accounting items such as liabilities, income, expenses, assets, equity, profit, and loss. The trial balance is used to determine the balance of credit and debit entries from the general ledger at a particular period.

The trial balance helps to adjust some entries in the general ledger. It is prepared to ensure that the total credits and debits are well balanced. The trial balance is not officially or legally required from businesses. It is only prepared for people within an organization and not be distributed to external parties.

The trial balance contains the entire accounts' total in the general ledger. Every account should have a description of the account, an account number, and its final credit or debit balance. Furthermore, the final date of the period the report is prepared should be included in the trial balance.

The primary difference between the general ledger and the trial balance is that the trial balance records the account totals from the general ledger, while the general ledger records all the transactions separately by account.

If any adjustments are to be made, it must show on a trial balance.

Errors That Can't Be Detected in a Trial Balance

Although a trial balance can reveal some inaccuracies of the general ledger, there are some errors this financial report cannot detect. These errors include:

An error of original entry: This occurs when the wrong amount is recorded on the debit and credit side.

An error of omission: This type of error occurs when the transaction is not recorded in the system.

Reversal error: This happens when a transaction is recorded with the correct amount, but the account meant to be credited is debited, while the one to be debited is credited.

Principle error: Principle error occurs when the transaction entered goes against the principles of accounting. For instance, the right amount is entered at the appropriate place, but the type of account the transaction recorded is wrong, e.g., using the asset account instead of the expense account.

Commission error: Commission error occurs when the amount of transaction is right, but the wrong account is credited or debited. Although commission errors may look like the error of principle, commission error occurs due to oversight and not a lack of knowledge.

How to Prepare a Trial Balance

Preparing a trial balance can be a challenging task for small business owners that already have the responsibility of recording their profits and losses, filing taxes returns, issuing invoices, and paying bills. Nevertheless, a trial balance is important for small businesses as it summarizes all the accounts of the general ledger and as well as detects errors in the ledger.

These days, technology advancements have made most accounting and bookkeeping tasks easier and faster to do. Accounting software can help you to prepare your trial balance; this accounting software helps you to remove errors made in the trial balance. The trial balance remains to be an important and useful financial document to businesses.

When preparing a trial balance, your general ledger is used to get the necessary information. The first step is that you separate credits from debits by accounts. A typical trial balance includes three columns: the accounts, debit side, and credit side. The debit side, which is on the left, can be represented with (DR) while the credit side (CR).

A trial balance uses the T-account. After setting up your format, then you will check the entries in the general ledger. You will enter the details from your general ledger into your trial balance. You need to list the name of the account and the amount of each account in the trial balance.

After doing this, you are required to add all the amounts on the debit side to derive the total debits. You can also adopt the same method to derive the total credit. If the credit total and the debit total are equal, your trial balance is well balanced. If the two totals do not match, your trial balance is unbalanced. According to the double-entry principle, your credit total must balance with your debit total.

If your trial balance is not balanced, you have to look for the reasons behind it. Once you detect the errors, you can then make necessary adjustments. You can detect errors by checking all the accounts included in your general ledger. The trial balance is as easy as that.

What a Working Trial Balance Is

Sometimes, a trial balance needs to be adjusted due to errors. When a business has a working trial balance, it refers to the account that is still worked on while making certain adjustments. The trial balance is referred to as a work-in-progress at that particular time. When the work-in-progress is accomplished, the result is referred to as an adjusted trial balance.

The adjusted trial balance is a balance sheet that has been updated after making some necessary adjustments to the account totals. Accountants prepare financial statements by utilizing the information on the adjusted trial balance.

To prepare a financial statement that is free from error, the first step is preparing a trial balance sheet and ensure that the credit and debit entries are equal. The trial balance is majorly prepared by business owners to reflect inaccuracies in financial records. When these errors are detected, the trial balance should be adjusted.

The T-account is used in preparing the trial balance, and it has the debit and credit sides. A working trial balance is a financial record in which adjustments are still being made.

Post-Closing Trial Balance

This is the last procedure in the preparation of a trial balance. The difference between post-closing trial balance and other trial balances is that the balance in the expense and income accounts must be zero. To decide the amount of income and expenses for a given period, one needs to begin with a Zero balance in the expense and income accounts.

With the post-closing trial balance, you can confirm if the balances of these accounts are zero. It also helps you to know if the debit amounts match with the credit amounts after you have closed the entries.

The Importance of a Trial Balance in Small Businesses

The importance of a trial balance cannot be underestimated. It is an important report for small businesses. As a business owner, anytime you prepare your general ledger, you need to check its accuracy. The trial balance helps you to accomplish this by:

Verifying the accuracy of your calculations

The trial balance helps you to check the accuracy of the general ledger. It ensures that the exact amount is recorded in the correct side, while posting the account's total from the different ledger books.

Helping you to prepare financial statements

The accounts in the ledger that are posted in the trial balance are further used for the preparation of financial statements, such as cash flow statement, income statement, and balance sheet. Therefore, the trial balance makes the preparation and analysis of these financial statements easier.

Helping your business to make a comparative analysis

With the trial balance in a business, a business can easily make a comparison between the current and past year balances. Such practices will enable a business to decide on its expenses, income, liabilities, and production costs. You can also take critical actions as long as you already have a clear picture of the present and past trends.

Detecting and correcting errors

In trial balance, the two totals of the two sides must be equal, i.e., the total on the debit side must be the same as the total on the credit side. If the two sides are not balanced, it reflects an inaccuracy. Accountants can detect and correct these errors.

Helping you to make adjustments

When preparing the trial balance, accounts such as outstanding liabilities, closing stock, prepaid expenses must be prepared. Doing this helps you to make the necessary adjustments in the current accounting year. At the end of each accounting year, businesses set up adjustment accounts.

Preparing an effective budget

The trial balance helps businesses make a comparison between the present and past ledger accounts. It also helps business owners follow or adjust the trend of their businesses' performance. After analyzing the performance of your business, you can then make budgets that will have a positive impact on your business.

Preparing audit reports

One of the financial experts that make use of the trial balance is the auditor. With the trial balance, auditors can easily identify the entries in the ledger. The trial balance provides an audit trail that is needed by auditors.

The trial balance summarizes all accounts in the ledger at the end of each accounting period. The trial balance is used for the preparation of trading profit and loss account and balance sheet.

The Difference Between the Trial Balance and Balance Sheet

- The trial balance verifies the accuracy of the calculations of the books of calculation, while the balance sheet reveals the exact financial position of a business.

- The trial balance is derived from the balances of all the accounts in the ledger, while the balance sheet contains the liabilities and assets accounts.

- Accountants prepare the trial balance before preparing the final accounts, while the balance sheet is prepared after the trading, profit and loss account has been prepared.

- The trial balance is used internally, while the balance sheet is used by external parties such as creditors, investors, etc.

- Trial balances can be prepared several times in an accounting period while balance sheets are prepared at the end of an accounting year.

CHAPTER 9

THE CASH BOOK AND CASH FLOW STATEMENT

All businesses make cash transactions. Cash is classified as a current asset of a business, used as a medium of exchange. Business transactions can be carried out by cash or on credit.

Currency notes and coins are examples of cash in accounting. The cash balance in a business is very important. This chapter explains how a cash book is prepared, the significance of a cash book in small businesses, and the types of cash books.

What is a Cash Book?

A cash book is a financial document that is used for recording payments made by cash. It is an essential account that records every cash transaction of business. It performs the function of a general ledger and a journal. The transactions related to cash payment and receipt are recorded in the cash book and then entered in the general ledger.

To have a better understanding of what the cash book does, we can explain the meaning of the two words, cash and book. Cash refers to an item that has monetary value like currency, coins, and checks. These items are used to pay for goods and services. In accounting, a book means a record of financial details that is in written form.

Therefore, the cash book records all financial transactions carried out with cash in a given period. The cash book records transactions carried out thorough checks and discounts given or received based on the type of cash book you prepare. The cash book is very useful for making accounting reports, tracking the flow of cash, and preparing taxes.

The Features of a Cash Book

To understand what a cash book is, one needs to know the features of a cash book. The features include:

- Dual entry: Like other accounting documents, a cash book has credit and debit entries. The debit entry reflects all increases in cash, while the credit entry reflects all transactions that lead to a decrease in cash.

- Performs the function of a journal and ledger: A cash book carries out the function of a general ledger and a journal.

- It must have a debit balance: The cash book records payments made by cash. Cash on hand helps to meet daily expenses in a business. Therefore, it is not possible to pay more than the cash in hand. As a result of this, the business will have a debit cash balance or no cash balance.

- Two equal sides: in accounting, the total of the debit entries of the cash book must be equal with the credit entries.

- Verifiable: The cash balance at the debit side can be re-checked by summing the cash in hand in the business.

Types of Cash Books

A cash book is designed based on the nature of a business and its requirements. A cashbook can be classified into two categories: general cash book and petty cash book.

General Cash Book

The general cash book first records cash transactions in a business and replace the ledger's cash account. The general cash book is divided into three classes.

Single Column Cash Book

The single-column cash book keeps track of all cash transactions. Cash payments are entered in the right column, while receipts will be recorded on the left column. This type of cash book does not keep track of bank transactions, discounts received, or discounts given.

Bank transactions and discounts are recorded in separate ledger accounts. Some businesses use a single column cash book. Cash books always have a debit balance and do not have a credit balance.

Double Column Cash Book

The double-column cash book keeps track of two kinds of transactions in two separate columns. There are two columns in this cash book. It records both cash transactions and discounts. Therefore, the discount given and received can be recorded in this cash book.

A discount is classified as a nominal account. Therefore, the discount received is regarded as a profit and is recorded on the credit side, while discounts given are recorded on the debit side because it is considered a loss.

Three Column Cash Book

The three-column cash book keeps track of cash, discount, and bank transactions. Most organizations use checks as a means of payment these days; therefore, a bank column included in your cash book makes work easier for you. The three-column cash book has a separate column where bank transactions are recorded.

If you received payment by check and the money is deposited the same day, the transaction is recorded on the debit side of the bank column. If the check was sent a day after the payment was received, it is recorded as a contra entry. A contra entry refers to the business transactions that occur between a bank account and a cash account.

Petty Cash Book

A petty cash book records several small cash transactions. Some transactions occur frequently, and these transactions are a small amount of money; therefore, the petty cash book keeps a record of such transactions. The person who manages a petty cash book is called a petty cashier.

Examples of transactions recorded in the petty cash book include food bills, postage, fuel expenses, stationery, cleaning, traveling, newspapers, office teas, etc. Petty transactions are often paid for using currency notes or coins. This type of cash book only records small transactions that are frequently made.

The petty cash book features a credit and debit side. Any payment is entered on the credit side, while receipts are entered on the debit side. In the general cash book, payment made for petty expenses are recorded on the credit side, but this is different in the petty cash book. Payment made for petty expenses are recorded on the petty cash book's debit side.

Elements of a Cash Book

You can understand a cash book by knowing its elements. The cash book has some elements that are explained below.

Date: In the cash book, the date of every transaction that occurs is recorded in the date column. The year is written on the top of the column.

Particulars: The particulars column of a cash book mentions the second account that is involved in a business transaction apart from cash. If the account is described with 'By,' the account is debited; it is credited if described with 'To.'

Voucher Number: If a business receives payment from a customer by cash, the business will give a receipt voucher. The number on the receipt voucher is recorded in front of the transaction made. When the business also makes a payment for any transaction, the business also receives a payment voucher. Receipt and payment vouchers are recorded in the Voucher Number Column.

Amount: The amount of the transaction made is recorded in two columns. In the cash book, the debit column records cash received, and the credit column records cash payments.

Bank: The bank column records all payments received or made by checks. Other types of bank transactions are also recorded in the bank column. The double-column cash book and three column cash book records bank transactions.

Discount: The discount column keeps records of discounts received and discounts allowed. Discount received is a discount given to a business when making purchases, while a discount allowed is a discount given to customers for the sale of a product. The discount allowed is recorded on the credit side of the discount column, while the discount received is recorded at the debit side of the discount column.

The Benefits of Cash Book

The cash book is very important in accounting and offers several benefits for business owners. Large and small business owners can use it. The type of cash book adopted depends on the type of business you operate.

If your business is a small one and you do not use checks or any other bank transactions, you can use the single column cash book. For large business owners that deal with bank transactions and also give and receive discounts, the three-column cash book or the two-column cash book can be used. The benefits of the cash book are discussed below.

- Keeps track of cash transactions: The cash book is a useful book of account that records all cash transactions in an organization.

- Determines cash present at hand: It helps you to know the amount of cash available in the organization.

- Records payments and receipts: This is another benefit of the cash book. With the cash book, you can determine cash payments made and cash receipts given at a particular date.

- Detects errors: With the cash book, you can easily detect errors by verifying the cash book balance. To verify the cash book, you can match the cash book balance with the exact cash in hand.

- Detects fraud: The cash book helps you detect theft or fraudulent practices carried out in your organization.

The Cash Flow Statement

The cash flow statement refers to a financial report that states the amount of cash earned and spent in a company. It reveals how cash is moving into and moving out of a business organization. It is also called the statement of cash flow; it is one of the primary financial statements used by financial analysts.

The cash flow statement reflects and evaluates how an organization manages its cash. It reveals how the performance of the balance sheet accounts and income statements influence the flow of cash. Accountants, shareholders, potential investors, analysts, employees, creditors, and contractors are the people interested in the statement of cash flow of an organization.

This financial statement is specifically designed to offer the necessary information on a business's solvency and liquidity. The cash flow statement is primarily concerned about how cash is generated and spent.

The Main Components of the Cash Flow Statement

The cash flow statement is divided into three major components, which are:

- The flow of cash from operating activities

- The flow of cash from investment

- The flow of cash from financing activities

The cash flow statement sometimes adds a disclosure of non-cash activities as part of the components according to the Generally Accepted Accounting Principles. The cash flow statement is different from the balance sheet account and the income statement.

Cash Flow from Operating Activities

Operating activities involve the manufacturing of goods, sales of goods, receiving payments from customers, and delivering the products of a company. These are activities that generate revenue for a business. These activities have to deal with purchases, sales, and expenses that will generate revenue for the business.

These expenses can be advertising, shipping the goods, purchasing raw materials, and building inventory. Cash flow from operating activities is the cash generated from the income of a company; it excludes costs related to investment in securities or investment on capital items.

The flow of cash from operating activities can be derived by using the direct and indirect method. The direct method reflects how the in-flow and out-flow of cash in the business affect all liability and current asset account. The indirect method reflects how profit is reconciled with cash flow.

Cash Flow from Investing Activities

Investing activities include loans given to suppliers, the sales of assets, purchases of assets, payments linked to acquisitions and mergers, and dividends received from another organization. Cash flow from investment refers to activities that are linked to the sale or purchase of capital assets.

Investing activities refer to activities that generate gain over a long-term period. They lead to changes in non-current assets like equipment, government bonds, investment in shares, etc. Investing activities have nothing to do with cash from external investors like shareholders or bondholders.

For instance, if a company pays out a dividend to its investors, this type of activity is not an investing activity; it is called a financing activity. Examples of investment activities include cash generated from selling an asset, cash spent on the purchase of an asset, cash generated as a result of the merger, cash generated from another company's acquisition.

Cash Flow from Financing Activities

Financing activities refer to events that lead to changes in the composition and size of the capital. Financing activities involve taking out loans, issuance of shares, paying dividends, etc. When a company extends credit to a customer, it is not a financial activity; it is an investing activity.

Cash flow related to repaying loans, borrowing, and issuing of shares is classified as cash flow from financing activities. Financing cash flow reveals the sale or purchase of stock in a company.

How to Calculate Cash Flow

In accounting, cash flow can be calculated by adjusting the net income. The operating cash flow is revealed in the statement of cash flow. The operating cash flow reflects the in-flow of cash during a particular period. There are two methods of calculating operating cash flow. These methods are direct and indirect.

The direct method derives information from the income statement by making use of cash disbursements and cash receipts. In the direct method, different kinds of payment received and made through cash are added. You can calculate these payments and receipts by making use of the balances of different business accounts.

In the indirect method, operating cash flow is calculated by deriving the net income from the income statement of an organization. Because the income statement of an organization is always made on an accrual basis, income is not recorded when it is received; it is recorded when it is earned. The indirect method is not a straightforward method of calculating operating cash flow.

The Importance of Cash Flow Statements

Investors are always concerned about the cash flow of an organization. Positive cash flow is a good sign for investors because this shows that the organization generates cash from its day-to-day operations. Operating cash flow can give a clear picture of an organization's profitability.

The purpose of preparing a statement of cash flow is to evaluate the sources of cash and how cash is utilized in a company over a particular period. The cash flow statement is one of the most important financial statements in accounting. Investors depend on this financial statement for making decisions because of its transparency.

The statement of cash flow helps to determine the solvency and liquidity of a business. It provides the necessary details for accessing a company's liabilities, assets, and equity. With the cash flow statement, businesses can determine the trends of their performance. This financial statement also predicts the timing and amount of cash flows in the future.

A business can only be successful if it has enough cash. Cash is needed to make business transactions like paying expenses, paying taxes, purchasing assets, and paying loans. With a cash flow statement, a business can determine the amount of cash available and how cash is generated and spent daily.

A business that lacks enough cash cannot make business transactions, and with time will go bankrupt. Without cash in a business, such businesses will need to borrow money to make some business transactions; this is not healthy for a business. The cash flow is useful in businesses and big organizations.

CHAPTER 10

THE INCOME STATEMENT ACCOUNT AND THE BALANCE SHEET

The income statement account and the balance sheets are one of the most important financial statements in accounting and bookkeeping. For all businesses, large or small, these financial statements are vital to evaluate and reflect your business's performance over a fiscal period. This chapter explains the uses of the income statement account and the balance sheet.

What is an Income Statement?

An income statement is a financial statement that reflects the profits, losses, income, and expenses of a business during a fiscal period. The income statement is also referred to as a profit and loss statement. The income statement is easy to understand since it states only the revenue and expenses accounts. This financial statement reflects the profitability of a business.

When revenues exceed expenses, the business is profitable. If expenses exceed revenue, the business is running at a loss.

The income statement is a crucial part of a business's financial statements. Used to list the income and expenses, it shows the net income and evaluates the business performance by analyzing non-operating and operating activities.

Investors use the income statement since it provides a clear picture of a business's profitability. This financial statement can influence investor's decisions. The income statements are required from large corporations because they provide users with the necessary details.

Why an Income Statement is Important

An income statement is important in businesses because of the following reasons:

Reflects the trends and patterns in business's finances. Since income statements are prepared monthly, quarterly, or yearly, companies can use them to compare past income statements with the present one. Comparison analysis can provide a great deal of information regarding the status of the company.

Provides a clear picture of a business's financial position: Income statements help businesses to determine their financial position. With this financial statement, you can easily know if your business is doing well or not.

Helps to make crucial decisions: The income statement is an important financial statement that helps business owners to make critical decisions. If your business is not doing well, you can plan strategies and make decisions that will improve your business's profitability.

Terms Used in Income Statements

Cost of Sales

The cost of sales states the cost of goods sold or services rendered by the business. Depreciation expenses are also included in the cost of sales. For businesses that produce goods, their cost of sales refers to the production of goods. It adds the expenses incurred from purchasing raw materials, labor, and manufacturing.

Retailers and wholesalers are also concerned about the cost of buying and reselling the products. Meanwhile, for businesses that render services, the cost of sales refers to the cost incurred from creating and rendering services to customers.

Net Sales

Net sales are the sales or income of a business. It reflects the sales of goods and services in a specified period. It reflects the profitability of a business.

Income Taxes

The income tax in the income statement is the estimation of income tax for the financial period.

Gross Income

It is also called gross margin or gross profit. The gross income is derived by calculating the difference between the cost of sales and net sales. Gross profit is the money available in a business that can be used to pay off expenses that might be incurred. The greater the gross profit, the more the net income.

Net Income

This is an important aspect of the income statement. The net income lists all operational and non-operational income and expenses and then calculates the difference. When income exceeds expenses, the business is running at a profit; if income is less than the expenses, the business is running at a loss.

Selling, General and Administrative Expenses

These expenses include the operational expenses incurred by the business. It reflects the business's efficiency. Business owners and investors are often more concerned about this aspect. If a business needs to cut its expenses, it considers the selling, general, and administrative expenses.

Operating Income

The operating income is derived by subtracting selling, general, and administrative expenses from the gross profit. Operating income is what the business can generate before deducting or adding any non-operating expenses.

Interest Expense

When a business borrows money, it will need to pay interest on the money borrowed. The interest expense refers to any interest payment made by the business.

Extraordinary Expenses

Sometime unexpected expenses arise in business. These occasional expenses need to be taken into account when planning a budget.

Understanding an Income Statement

There are certain things you need to know when analyzing and interpreting the income statement. The income statement will reveal everything about a business's profitability. As a business owner, accountant, and bookkeeper, you need to make sure the figures in this statement are accurate. Ensure your calculations are correct, because any mistake made will affect the evaluation of the business.

It is important to know the indicators that matter most and evaluate them carefully. One of the indicators that helps determine the profitability of a business is gross income. The operating income shows the efficiency of your business in terms of management. The net income is one of the major concerns for investors as it reveals the overall profitability of your business.

As a business owner or an investor, you might decide to compare the results of your income statement with another business that runs the same type of business. Comparing the income statements of business organizations can reveal how your business is performing in the industry.

Small businesses might find it difficult to have access to income statements of other similar businesses. Some businesses offer a financial statement that can give crucial information about the status of the company. The accounting methods adopted by businesses can influence the income statement. For instance, some businesses make use of the cash basis method, which records revenue when businesses receive cash.

There can be differences in the expenses section too. The way expenses are accounted for can influence the annual expenses of a business. When comparing and analyzing income statements, you must figure out where the different methods are utilized in order to have a better overview of the company.

The Balance Sheet

The balance sheet is one of the most essential financial statements in accounting. It is crucial to understanding the performance of a business. This financial statement reflects the net worth of a business. It is a financial statement that states the asset, liability, and equity of a business. The accounting equation: Assets $=$ Liabilities $+$ Equity is the basis of the balance sheet.

There are two main sides in the balance sheet: the right and the left side. The owner's equity, as well as the liabilities recording, are done on the right-hand side, while the left side takes an accounting of the company's assets. Assets are classified into fixed and current assets, while liabilities are current and long-term liabilities. This financial statement gives you a clear picture of your small business's financial position at a particular period.

The Structure of the Balance Sheet

The balance sheet follows a particular structure. There are several items included in the balance sheet. These items are explained below.

Current Assets

Cash and cash equivalents: In the balance sheet, assets are recorded on the left side. Cash, which is an example of current assets, is recorded first. Other assets recorded in this section include cash equivalents and other assets that are short term or assets that can be liquidated, like marketable securities.

Inventory: The inventory account involves the amounts for goods still in the production process, raw materials, and finished products. Inventories are goods manufactured or purchased by a company to be sold to customers. From the time of production to the time they are purchased by customers, it is known as inventory.

Accounts receivable: Accounts receivable refer to the amount debtors are yet to pay a business organization. It refers to the sales revenue that have not yet been received from customers or debtors.

Fixed Asset

Fixed assets are also known as non-current assets. They refer to the physical assets that a business owns. Fixed assets depreciate with time; therefore, when these assets are recorded, a depreciation amount is deducted from them.

Equipment, property, and plants: Property, equipment, and plants fall into this category. Examples include land, buildings, vehicles, and other types of equipment. Land is a good example of fixed assets that are owned for a longer period than other types of fixed assets. It is a type of fixed asset whose value does not depreciate but tends to appreciate over time.

Intangible Asset

Intangible asset refers to assets of a company that adds value to that company. Such assets are not easily valued. Examples include licenses, goodwill, patents, and secret formulas.

Current Liabilities

Current liabilities are also referred to as short term liabilities. These liabilities are obligations that have to be made within a short period of time.

Accounts payable: Accounts payable refer to the amount owed by a company. When a company buys stocks, items, or services on credit from another supplier, it is called account payable. This type of liability has to be paid back within a short term. When a business pays off its debt, the cash account decreases as well as the accounts payable.

Accrued expenses: These are listed as liabilities in the bookkeeping, but the due date has not come. Examples include wages, interest, etc.

Taxes payable: Many companies owe local, state and federal tax. When a business owes taxes that were meant to be paid to the government, it is called taxes payable. All taxes are classified as current liabilities since they are to be paid within a year.

Non-Current Liabilities

This is also called long term liabilities. This term refers to debts that will be due in more than a year. There are debts whose payments are extended over a long period. It refers to the amount of money a company owes a third party, and it becomes due to be paid for more than one year.

Bonds payable: Bonds payable refer to the number of bonds a company issues, and it is yet to be paid.

Long-term debt: This is also a good example of non-current liabilities. It is the total amount owed by a company, and it is not yet to be paid. This account is obtained from the debt schedule and reflects all the outstanding debt owed by a business.

Owner's Equity

This is also referred to as shareholder's equity. It is the amount of money that the business owner invests in the business. When a business starts, the owner will invest money for the smooth running of the business; such amount is called the owner's equity. It is derived by deducting total liabilities from total assets.

Retained earnings: This refers to the net income a business keeps. In every financial period, a business may decide to pay off dividends from the net income. The amount left is added to retained earnings. This also refers to the excess earnings kept back by the business.

How is the Balance Sheet Interpreted and Analyzed

The balance sheet is a financial statement used by business owners, investors, and financial analysts. A financial analyst can use this financial statement to derive financial ratios that will help to evaluate the financial performance of a business.

The changes in this financial statement can be used to derive cash flow in the statement of cash flow. For instance, a positive change in fixed assets like machinery, plant, and the property is equal to capital expenses less depreciation expense.

Importance of Balance Sheet

The balance sheet is a very vital financial statement in accounting. This section discusses the importance of the balance sheet in businesses.

It is an important document used by stakeholders, investors, and creditors to have an insight into the financial position of a business.

It can be used to make a comparison between organizations in the same sector; this will help to evaluate the growth of a business.

Since the balance sheet states the assets, liabilities, and equity of a business, it reveals the solvency and liquidity of a business.

By comparing the past and present balance sheet of an organization, it enables an organization to identify the pattern of growth. Identifying the pattern of growth helps the organization make decisions that will improve business activity.

It can be used to determine how a business generates returns. For instance, when the net income is divided into the owner's equity, it is Return on Equity (ROE). When net income is divided into total assets, it generates Return on Assets (ROA).

- The analysis of the balance sheet can enable a business to undertake some projects and meet unplanned expenses.

- The balance sheet also helps to determine if a business is being funded with debt or profit. Hence, it reveals the profitability of a business.

The Difference Between the Income Statement and Balance Sheet

Although the income statement and the balance sheet are both financial statements, these two financial statements are different. The differences between these two statements are discussed below.

Items recorded: The income statement accounts for revenue and expenses that lead to calculating net gain or loss, while the balance sheet accounts for assets, liability, and shareholder's equity.

Uses: The income statement is used to evaluate the profitability of a business, i.e., if a business is running at a profit or loss. The balance sheet helps to evaluate the liquidity of a business.

Timing: the balance sheet reflects the financial position of a business at a particular period while the income statement reflects the results of a business for a longer period. For instance, financial statements for December will have a profit and loss statement for December and a balance sheet as of December 31.

Metrics: sales are compared with the subtotals in the profit and loss statement to generate the operating income percentage, gross profit percentage, and net income percentage. The different items recorded in the balance sheet are compared to determine a business's liquidity.

The balance sheet and the profit and loss statement are important to understanding how a business operates and determining the liquidity of a business. Small business owners can prepare the profit and loss statement as well as the balance sheet to check the growth of their businesses.

The structures of the balance sheet and the items reported in it have been explained in this chapter. The profit and loss statement are also easy to prepare. Regardless of the type or nature of your business, the income statement and the balance sheet are important.

CHAPTER 11

CASH FLOW MANAGEMENT IN SMALL BUSINESSES

Small businesses need to manage the flow of cash in their businesses, as this is a vital aspect of business management. This chapter discusses how cash, accounts payable and accounts receivable can be managed in small businesses.

What is Cash?

Cash is a very useful asset in a business, and it is the most liquid asset. It performs several functions in a business. No matter the type or nature of a business, cash is needed. Cash plays a significant role in running a business. Cash is used for the following purposes:

Transactions: Cash is used to make business transactions; without cash, no business transaction can be carried out. No matter the type of payments made, either by cash, checks, credit card, cash is always needed.

Security: Cash available in a business guarantees the security of the business. The amount of cash available in a business reflects its solvency.

Investment: No matter the type or nature of the investment, cash is needed for investments.

Cash is needed to meet the needs of a business. Most transactions carried out in businesses involve cash. Transactions that do not involve cash are non-financial. Business owners become more concerned when the cash available in the business is not enough to carry out business transactions. This is can be risky because most businesses that lack cash often end up taking out bank loans or borrowing from other businesses and going deeper into debt.

However, it is not only cash scarcity that occurs in businesses, but the surplus of cash is also a concern for businesses. Some businesses experience cash surplus, but they do not know what to do with the surplus.

It is financially unhealthy to leave cash surplus in accounts without investing it on something profitable for your business. Excess cash can generate income for your business if you use them wisely. Since cash is a liquid asset, it can be easily be converted and managed.

How to Use Excess Cash?

If you have excess cash in your business, it can be used for several things including:

Treasury Securities

The Treasury obligations of the United States is the biggest sector of the money market. Bonds are the primary securities issued here.

Commercial Paper

Commercial paper is a promissory note that has a fixed maturity. Financial organizations and certain companies issue commercial paper. It can be bought through dealers or directly from the finance organizations. Companies like CIT Financial Corporation sell commercial paper. Companies issue commercial paper at a discount.

Banker's Acceptances

These are drafts used in financing domestic and international trade. Banks accept these drafts, and their creditworthiness is determined by the acceptance of the draft by the bank. Banker's acceptances are traded in a market where few dealers dominate.

Agency Securities

The federal government has several agencies, and their duties are guaranteed by agency security. The Government National Mortgage Association (GNMA) and the Federal Housing Administration (FHA) are the primary agencies in charge of issuing securities. The securities issued are highly marketable.

Cash Inflow and Cash Outflow

What is Cash Inflow?

A business can generate cash through the sale of fixed assets, new debt, new investment, and operating income. The most reliable source of cash inflow is operating profits. The backbone of a business is the payment receipt from customers for rendering services or selling products. When customers make a payment for selling your products or services immediately, more cash will be generated in the business.

Cash can be managed efficiently when customers make a payment without delays. An example of this ideology is the fast-food industry. In the fast-food industry, payments are made by credit card or cash. Payments made by checks have to go through a process that can be time-consuming. It takes some time for banks to clear a check; therefore, payments made by check are not prompt payments.

The objective of cash management is to reduce the time it takes for funds to be transferred. Several techniques have been developed to speed up the check's clearance.

Lockboxes: A lockbox system can be used by businesses to collect payments. If you want to do this, you need to rent a post office box. Then you have to inform your bank to open the lockbox and credit your account directly.

Concentration banking: Large businesses can have wide market coverage. You can make use of banks at different locations to accelerate the process of clearing checks. This will help transfer funds faster.

The concentration of cash: When cash is concentrated in an account, it allows you to reduce cash reserves.

What is Cash Outflow?

Cash outflow refers to the amount of money disbursed by a business. It is the amount of money that leaves a business. It can be as a result of paying wages, paying dividends, and paying rent. When a business's cash outflow exceeds its inflow, this is financially unhealthy for such a business.

Cash outflows are a result of expenses incurred in the business. A business should ensure that it considers the type of demands it makes on its cash.

Cash Flow Budgets

You must prepare a cash flow analysis before you make a cash flow budget. A cash flow analysis helps you evaluate the inflow and outflow of cash in your business. A cash flow analysis gives you a clear picture of how your business operates. Small businesses need to understand how cash flows work. Small businesses are sometimes vulnerable to cash flow problems because they tend to perform business transactions with insufficient cash reserves or none.

Businesses must consider the time cash flows in and out. For instance, if a business spends cash in the first half of the year and generates cash in the second half of the year, it might fail before it is has a chance to receive cash inflows to operate well. Cash flow timing is very important in business.

Many small businesses fail to control the flow of cash. Preparing a cash flow budget is very important for businesses that want to control their cash flow. Businesses can get into trouble if they lack enough cash to pay their bills. Managing the flow of cash in your business is not a complex thing to do.

You only need some systematic approaches to control cash flow in your business. You need to do the following:

Determine the Sources of Cash In-Flows in Your Business

The sources of cash inflows include new debts and new investments. However, you cannot depend on these sources because they are not frequent. When you sell fixed assets, they are examples of new investments. Selling fixed assets are secondary to operating profits. For businesses, it is crucial to pay attention to operating profits.

Operating profits are not easy to track because they are ongoing. Therefore, businesses need to monitor their operating profits constantly. As your business grows, the need for cash will increase. For instance, when a business is experiencing fast growth, it will need to increase its inventory, cash transactions, and receivables. The process of increasing inventory will likely require large amounts of cash.

The period when businesses experience fast growth may be a challenging one. During these periods, receivables, inventories, etc. might consume all your gains. Some of these problems might result from extending payment terms to clients while you are being asked to pay suppliers within a short period.

Identify Cash Outflows

You can identify how cash is going out by checking the cash journal. It is important to identify where you are spending the cash. When disbursing cash in the business, it is important to ask questions like, "Is the expenditure necessary?" "Is the timing right?" "Can the expenditure be postponed?" If you cannot identify where you are spending cash, you need to consult an accountant. Small businesses can get enough details of cash disbursements from a checkbook.

Identify the Timing of Cashflow and Distribution

A calendar helps you to determine the timing of cash flow. Since most businesses prepare accounts yearly, you can examine your income and expenditures in a year. Before you do this, you need to make a list of cash outflow. List the items you have spent money on until you are certain that the list is complete. When you are done listing cash outflow, you can start listing cash inflow. This will give you a clear picture of cash flow timing.

Examine the Difference Between the Outflow of Cash and The In-Flow of Cash

When cash inflow exceed cash outflow, it is called a positive cash flow period. If a business experiences positive cash flow, such a business is successful. But this may not be the case at all times, as there are cases where cash outflow exceeds cash inflow. If a business experiences a negative cash flow period, it will need to source funds from other sources, such as a borrowing money from a bank.

Sometimes, negative cash flow occur in businesses, especially when growth spurts occur. Some businesses go through a period of sales rhythms. If this happens, observe the rhythm and the timing of cash inflow so that you can plan well for negative cash flow when it occurs.

Identify How the Present Cash Flow Affects the Business

One of the ways a business owner can regulate and improve cash flow is to reduce the outflow of cash while accelerating the inflow of cash. Before you do this, you need to evaluate the effects of slowing down payment to suppliers.

Identify the Sources of Outflow and Inflow Whose Timings Can be Altered

To prevent negative cash flow conditions, you can identify the cash outflow and cash inflow that can be altered. Sometimes, you need to discuss this with your creditors and decide on a payment schedule that is helpful to you. Some large companies and banks will agree on payment schedules as long as it benefits the parties involved.

If you inform your creditors that payment cannot be made at a particular period, they can reschedule their cash flow requirements.

Set Up a Strategy for Positive Cash Flow

A cash budget is a tool for planning positive cash flows. Cash budget refers to making plans for cash needs and cash receipts in the future. A cash budget reflects the amount and timing of cash that will be generated and disbursed over a specified period. For instance, most businesses prepare a budget for a year; you can prepare a two-year cash budget by making changes to the budget of the second year.

The cash budget should consider seasonal variations in cash flows. You need to know that the longer your cash flow budget is, your projections become more uncertain. The essence of a cash budget is to make plans for cash outflow and inflow that might occur in the future; the accuracy of your projection makes it useful.

How to Prepare Cash Budgets

To prepare cash budgets for a business, one needs to make sales projections. When generating a sales projection, you can ask the sales manager to forecast sales for the future. The sales manager observes the trends and patterns of sales in your business and then derives these estimates. This approach of making sales projections is the internal approach.

Since the internal approach may be too narrow, many businesses utilize the external approach of making sales projections. Some consulting organizations utilize an econometric modeling approach to estimate economic conditions. Another step you need to take when preparing a cash budget is to identify the cash receipts. The past trends of your credit and cash sales should be used to determine time delays.

CHAPTER 12

FINANCING YOUR SMALL BUSINESS

As a small business owner, you need to pay attention to your business financing. All businesses, whether large or small, needs finance; it is a vital aspect of a business. When talking about business financing, one needs to make a clear difference between new businesses and the ones that have existed for some time. This chapter talks about business financing and how small business owners can finance their businesses by going bankrupt.

What is Business Finance?

When we talk about business finance, we mean the money and credit channeled to a business for its smooth operations. It refers to acquitting and utilizing funds so that a business can perform day-to-day operations. Business finance involves all kinds of funds used for a business's operations. Regardless of the type, size, and nature of a business, finance is needed every time.

Finance is the lifeblood of a business; without it, no business can exist. The amount used for funding a business differs from one business organization to another based on the type, size, and nature of the business. Therefore, business finance has to do with the raising of funds, investment of funds, and estimation of funds.

One of the major problems small businesses face is the lack of funds. Some businesses have closed down because of a lack of funds. Running a business is not meant for people who are weak at heart, but for those who are willing to take a risk. Starting a business is a risk.

Small Business Financing

Most small businesses fund their business operations using traditional small business loans. These loans are useful when starting a business; it helps to build working capital and create cash flow. Small business financing may need to be funded by personal loans as well as small business loans. Small business owners need to be very careful when taking out a loan from entities because some may result in bad credit loans.

Large businesses have more access to financing than small businesses because large businesses tend to have more assets that are mostly used as collateral to secure loans. These assets can be sold off when the business cannot pay back any monies owed. Therefore, lenders always know that large businesses can look for ways to pay back the loan.

Larger businesses have more experience and longer operational history. Lenders always check the operating history of a business before considering granting it a loan. The operation history of businesses reveals a lot about the business because it reflects the profitability of the business and is the main reason lenders require for it before granting loans.

Although large businesses might have more opportunities to take out bank loans than small businesses do, there are several kinds of loans for small businesses too. Small business owners should not borrow large amounts of money to fund their businesses; this might be very risky, especially if it can't be paid back.

The Need to Finance a Business

For any organization, firm, or business to stand strong, it requires funding. Funds are required for the purchase of land, machinery, inventory, etc.

Money is also required for paying wages and salaries, utility bills, interest expenses, rents, telephone bills, etc. In the business world, the process of production continues because goods or services will be demanded. Businesses will continue to incur expenses. Funds will help a business to achieve lots of things; for example, an organization might need to purchase computers to be installed in offices. In this case, funds are required.

Funds are needed to meet unforeseen expenses that might occur in businesses. Funds are also required to boost sales. A business organization might need to adopt strategies like home delivery service, advertising, personal selling, etc. to boost sales. Such a business needs money to accomplish these tasks.

Funds are also needed to make good use of business opportunities that may arise in businesses. Suppose there is a sales offer for a business, a supplier promises to give a 20% discount if it buys goods worth $150,000. This is considered a big opportunity for the business, but it will not be able to make good use of such an opportunity if it lacks funds.

Funds are needed to finance a business's inventory. Once a business organization is established, it needs money to manufacture its own goods or to purchase inventory. An organization invests a whole lot on purchasing or manufacturing inventory before it starts receiving payment for the inventory sold.

Types of Business Finance

One of the primary reasons businesses fail is lack of capital. It is not easy to run a business. In the financial year 2017/2018, more than 250,000 businesses failed. This can be a result of insufficient investment in operations. Therefore, you must choose the type of finance that is suitable for your business. This decision is critical to running a successful or a failed business.

A business can either be financed with debt or equity. Therefore, there are two primary types of business finance: equity finance and debt finance. A business is debt-financed when funds are borrowed from an external entity and paid back with interest, while a business financed with equity receives funds from the shareholder and use it to run a business.

What is Debt Financing?

In the financing world, a business is funded by debt when it borrows money from external parties with an agreement to pay back at a specified date. Small business loans, term loans, credit cards, and merchant cash advance are examples of debt financing. The loans granted to small businesses can be short term or long term.

The short-term loan spans 30 days to 12 months, while long term loans span one year to five years. If your business is financed by debt, your business is still owned by you, unlike equity financing that affects the ownership of your business.

Before an institution or entity can grant you a loan, the creditworthiness of your business will be evaluated by lenders. They will consider the financial records of your business, your operation history, credit rating, ability to pay back the loan, and if you have invested in the business. Debt financing has its advantages and disadvantages.

Pros:

- You have absolute control over your business.

- You have the capital to start your business with an agreement to pay back at a specified date.

- The loan can either be a short term or long-term loan.

- It is suitable for business owners as there are many sources of debt financing.

166

- The loans' interest is tax-deductible.

Cons:

- You have to pay back the loan at a specified time.

- The repayments of the loan start immediately after the loan approval.

- Cash inflow needs to be sufficient and steady to pay back at the agreed time.

- There is a probability that the business might not be able to pay back due to some unexpected happenings.

- The loan is always granted and secured against collateral.

- The business might not be able to grow again because the loan repayment drained some cash.

Sources of Debt Finance

There are various sources of debt finance; the primary sources are explained below.

Retailers: You can finance your business by buying goods on credit for your business. Several small businesses do that. Some retailers are ready to offer you goods with no interest.

Relatives or friends: Your family member(s) or friends can offer you a loan with an agreement that you will repay it at a particular date.

Financial institutions: These include credit unions and banks. They can provide you with lines of credit, bank overdrafts, and loans. Banks offer to provide funds for your business by granting loans to you. The bank offers you a particular amount of money with an agreement to repay the loan over a specified period.

A line of credit is like a credit card that provides a facility that you can use when you need it and pay it back on an agreed term. Business owners can have issues in getting a line of credit or a bank loan. The bank is only interested in being repaid with interest. Banks grant loans and expect borrowers to pay interest on the loan.

Finance companies: Finance companies provide loans to businesses.

Peer-to-peer lenders: This kind of entity matches people who need loans with people who have funds to invest. Loans granted have to be paid back within a specific period, and the rates of interest differ based on the level of risk involved.

Factor companies: Factoring is a process in which a business organization sells its accounts receivable to a third entity, which is referred to as a factor to receive funds without having to wait for customer payment. Invoices are paid by customers to the factoring company directly.

Invoice financing: This happens when your invoices are exchanged for upfront cash that is equal to a percentage of the value of your invoice. This is ideal for your business if it struggles with the differences between payment and invoices.

Trade finance: This is a type of finance that is utilized for the facilitation of exports and imports.

What is Equity Financing?

Equity financing is when a third-party investor is funding a business, and a percentage of that business is bought or owned by the investor. The investor offers you the capital needed, and he has a share in the profit earned in the business. The investor can also take part in the decision-making process.

For the investor, equity financing comes with a high level of risk. If the business fails, the investor will be paid back. There are several factors to consider in equity financing, and this includes voting rights, decision making, dilution, and the valuation and exit methods. Equity financing comes with some benefits and disadvantages:

Pros:

- It involves less risk since the amount invested need not be repaid immediately.

- There will be more cash available in the business since you don't need to pay back a loan.

- The skills and credibility of investors can be favorable to your operation.

- Funds can be raised at an early stage without having an operating history, unlike loans that require the profitability of a business or its operating history.

Cons:

- The ownership of your business is affected as investors take a share of your business's ownership.

- Investors take part in the decision-making process.

- The process of getting investors who will be interested in your business is time-consuming and challenging. It requires legal considerations and intricate contracts.

Sources of Equity Finance

The primary sources of equity finance include the following:

Venture capital: This is a type of business that deals with investing in businesses in whom they see profits and potentials.

Government: Sometimes, the government encourages small business owners by granting them funds to start their businesses. This can come in the form of information and guidance and low cost or free advisory services.

Private investors: Private investors are called 'business angels.' These "angels" are wealthy and invest a large amount of money in businesses to have a share of the profits as well a share of the ownership.

Family or friends: Your family member(s) or friends can fund your business in exchange for taking a share of your business profits and ownership. You need to be careful in accepting this offer as it may result in creating an unhealthy relationship with your friends or family.

Crowdfunding: This refers to raising funds via the collective endeavors of a group of people. Examples include crowdfunding platforms or social media. It allows investors to offer a large amount of money in return for profit or ownership.

Personal finances: This is very common in small businesses. When the business owner decides to fund the business from her personal assets or personal savings, it is personal finance. Business owners are advised against using home loans, retirement savings, and insurance loans to fund risky businesses.

Angel investors: These set of people are interested in investing in a profitable business by purchasing equity. They can provide funds, advice, and expertise to help you start a business and make it grow. Angel investors are very hard to come by because they always require evaluating the profitability and viability of a business plan.

They always have an exit plan. An exit plan is a strategy that allows investors to get their money back and take their profits. Often, these investors operate on a limited time frame, which can be within three to five years.

Types of Finance

The types of finance in this section are defined based on the duration period of its operating cycle, and its purpose. There are three types of finance - short-term, medium-term, and long-term.

Short-Term Finance

Short-term finance is for use within a year. This type of finance is needed for financing the daily operations of a business.

Medium-Term Finance

Businesses use this finance for more than a year, but not more than five years. The medium-term finance is needed for renovation, repair, and modernization of machinery.

Long-Term Finance

Long-term finance has a duration of about five years or more before being repaid. This type of finance is needed for financing and the purchase of non-current or fixed assets such as machinery, land, vehicles, etc.

CHAPTER 13

CLOSING THE BOOKS FOR YEAR-END

In bookkeeping and accounting, a business has to close its books for the year-end. At the beginning of the year, different financial statements are prepared, and at the end of the year, these accounts and statements need to be closed. This chapter discusses how books are closed for the year-end.

What Does a Closing Process Mean?

A closing process in accounting refers to the steps an accountant must take to review and zero out some accounts, like the income and expenses accounts, and then record the net profit or loss in the balance sheet. If you use accounting software to prepare your books, it will close your revenue and expense accounts automatically.

Most times, the closing process is always carried out by an accountant. However, a small business owner can use accounting software to accomplish this task. Your books need to be closed annually since you need to file income tax returns every year. It is a common practice among businesses to close their books monthly.

If you perform many transactions and your business is large, you might need to leave the closing process to your accountant. As a business owner, you should understand the process of closing the books, even if you are not doing it yourself. This will help you to know if your job was well done.

Closing your books for the year-end means that all your reports have been finalized. These reports reveal the financial performance of a business during an accounting period. Business owners are entitled to know the ups and downs of their business.

Closing entries are aspects of the accounting process that occur at the end of an accounting period. During the closing process, balances in temporary accounts are posted to permanent ones. These temporary accounts include dividends, income, and expense accounts.

Why You Need to Close Your Books

There are different reasons you need to close your books. The main purpose of closing the books is to ensure that revenue generated and expenses incurred from a previous accounting year are not carried over to the current account year. The closing process also helps business owners have insight into the financial position of their business.

Small business owners should ensure that their books are closed at the end of the year to file income tax returns annually. When you close your books, you can easily detect any error in your bookkeeping and accounting system. Closing the books also help businesses prepare for the next accounting period.

When you close your books monthly, it makes it easier to carry out monthly tasks such as paying your suppliers, sending invoices to customers, reconciling bank statements, preparing the journal, and sending reports on sales tax to the state. The closing process also helps you create an outline and strategies for the next accounting period.

Steps You Need to Take When Closing the Books

Transfer Entries in the Journal to the General Ledger

The journal is the first book where transactions are recorded. Entries in the journal need to be posted to the general ledger. The closing process requires you to record the account totals from your cash receipts and payments in the general ledger. Cash payments involve all transactions paid with cash or checks.

Add Up All Accounts in the General Ledger

This is the second step you need to take when you are closing the books. Sum up all the transactions in every general ledger account. For instance, you can sum up all entries in the expense account.

Prepare a Preliminary Trial Balance

A trial balance is a financial report that calculates all debits and credits of your accounts. Ensure the debits and credits are balanced and if it is not the case, recheck your work to correct the errors.

Adjusting Entries

Adjusting entries keep track of items that are not recorded as daily transactions. These items are accrual of depreciation, accumulation of taxes.

Adjust the Trial Balance Again

Add up all accounts in your general ledger again to check the adjusting entries and total them to prepare a new trial balance.

Make Financial Reports

If you discover out that the total credits and debits are the same in your trial balance, then you can prepare your profit and loss statement and balance sheet. You can prepare these financial reports with your accounting software. Accounting software makes the preparation of financial statements easier and faster.

Make Closing Entries

This step requires you to zero your income and expense accounts and then enter the net loss of income to the owner's equity. Closing entries record the balances of these accounts to permanent accounts. For instance, the income account is cleared out and transferred into the retained earnings account.

Create a Post-Closing Trial Balance

Creating a post-closing trial balance is the last procedure in closing the books for the year-end. The difference between post-closing trial balance and other trial balances is that the balance in the expense and income accounts must be zero. To decide the amount of income and expenses for a particular period, one needs to begin with a zero balance in the expense and income accounts.

The trial balance will only include the balance sheet since all expenses and income accounts have been cleared out. Ensure that the credit and debit balances are the same in your prepared trial balance.

What You Need to Consider When Closing Your Books

There are several things you need to take into account when closing your books. The steps on how to close your books has been discussed above, but you need to know some things about closing your books.

Reconciliation of your bank account: Ensure that the balance on your books is the same with your final financial reports, especially if you have been recording transactions by hand. Remember, humans make mistakes. Be certain that all credit cards, money accounts, and bank statements are reconciled properly.

If you utilize accounting software make sure you crosscheck all the figures. If you want to be sure that your bank accounts are reconciled, you can employ a team of experts to make the work less stressful for you.

Evaluate Invoices and Accounts Receivable

Be certain that your invoices at the end of the year are cleared, and all invoices sent out are remunerated. Sent invoices can go unnoticed due to several tasks been performed at the year-end. This can lead to errors in your books. Therefore, you need to pay attention to all the details and make sure all transactions are well recorded.

Check Income Statements and Payroll Expenses

During the closing process, ensure that your annual and monthly payroll expenses are balanced. You need to check income statements and payroll expenses before filing your yearly taxes.

If you fail to deal with payroll expenses properly, you can be penalized by the IRS. Also, you need to have a careful study of your income statements to ensure that it is well arranged. You can seek help from a professional if you are not certain about your payroll taxes.

Fixed Assets and Depreciation Expenses

Things you need to take into account are your depreciation expenses and fixed assets when closing your book for the year-end. If you purchased any fixed assets, make sure you keep good track of them in your balance sheets. Deal with problems associated with depreciation during the closing process. This can be a little bit tricky and might need the skill of a professional.

The Accounts Affected by Closing Entries

Closing entries affect some accounts like revenue accounts, dividend accounts, and expense accounts. These accounts are cleared out when closing entries. Closing entries alter these accounts so that they don't change the next accounting period.

The balances of these accounts are recorded in retained earnings, which is not a temporary account. Sometimes, income and expenses are posted to an income summary, while dividends are posted to retained earnings.

CONCLUSION

You can only evaluate the performance of your businesses if you practice the art of bookkeeping and accounting. Bookkeeping and accounting help to organize your finances and evaluate your business's performance. As a business owner, you must have a financial understanding of how your business operates. A good bookkeeping and accounting system helps you to plan for the future.

Accounting and bookkeeping are very vital for operating a business. They are used in many organizations, and their principles apply to daily business operations. Every business spends money and makes sales, and with accounting and bookkeeping, it is easy to track these transactions. Regardless of the type or size of your business, accounting and bookkeeping play a significant role.